PRAISE FOR *SABBATH*

"I am in awe of the wonder of Wayne Muller. His wisdom and his compassion resonate with the highest feelings in my soul. I am deeply moved by the profound insights in *Sabbath*."

—Neale Donald Walsch, bestselling
author of *Conversations with God*

"Wayne Muller's wonderfully soothing book gives us permission to rest, reflect, and appreciate. And he gives us many spiritual tools to guide us. In a world of enormous stress, can there be a more valuable gift?"

—Susan Jeffers, Ph.D., author of *End the Struggle and Dance with Life* and *Feel the Fear and Do It Anyway*

"*Sabbath* is a valuable guide in bringing a sense of sacredness to the hectic pace of modern life. Muller writes with the simplicity and elegance typical of great spiritual insights."

—Larry Dossey, M.D., author
of *Prayer Is Good Medicine*

"With the passion of a poet and the meticulousness of a scholar, Muller gathers up the wisdom of the world's spiritual traditions about rest and reminds us that dormancy is part of the natural way life deepens and grows. *Sabbath* might be described in many ways; it is wise, profound, lyrical, radical, and insightful. But most of all, this book is anointed."

—Rachel Naomi Remen, M.D.,
author of *Kitchen Table Wisdom*

"In *Sabbath*, Wayne Muller gives us the license, the encouragement to take that single mindful breath which puts our busy lives in perspective and helps restore our souls. 'Downward mobility,' Henri Nouwen counseled! Wayne believed Henri and helps his readers to grow in this essential understanding."

—Fred Rogers, of *Mister Rogers' Neighborhood*

Restoring the Sacred Rhythm
of Rest

SABBATH

Wayne Muller

BANTAM BOOKS

New York Toronto London Sydney Auckland

SABBATH: RESTORING THE SACRED RHYTHM OF REST

A Bantam Book / April 1999

Book design by Dana Leigh Treglia.

Library of Congress Cataloging-in-Publication Data
Muller, Wayne, 1953–
Sabbath : restoring the sacred rhythm of rest / Wayne Muller.
p.   cm.
ISBN 0-553-10672-4
1. Rest—Religious aspects—Christianity.   2. Sabbath.   3. Christian life.
I. Title.
BV4509.5.M84   1999
291.3′6—dc21   98-43982
                                                                                    CIP

Published simultaneously in the United States and Canada

Bantam Books are published by Bantam Books, a division of Random House, Inc. Its trademark, consisting of the words "Bantam Books" and the portrayal of a rooster, is Registered in U.S. Patent and Trademark Office and in other countries. Marca Registrada. Bantam Books, 1540 Broadway, New York, New York 10036.

PRINTED IN THE UNITED STATES OF AMERICA

BVG   10 9 8 7 6 5 4 3 2 1

For Henri Nouwen
my teacher and my friend

Contents

TIME

HAPPINESS

WISDOM

CONSECRATION

A SABBATH DAY

Remember the Sabbath

In the relentless busyness of modern life, we have lost the rhythm between work and rest.

All life requires a rhythm of rest. There is a rhythm in our waking activity and the body's need for sleep. There is a rhythm in the way day dissolves into night, and night into morning. There is a rhythm as the active growth of spring and summer is quieted by the necessary dormancy of fall and winter. There is a tidal rhythm, a deep, eternal conversation between the land and the great sea. In our bodies, the heart perceptibly rests after each life-giving beat; the lungs rest between the exhale and the inhale.

We have lost this essential rhythm. Our culture invariably supposes that action and accomplishment are better than rest, that doing something—anything—is better than doing nothing. Because of our desire to succeed, to meet these ever-growing expectations, we do not rest. Because we do not rest, we lose our way. We miss the compass points that would show us where to go, we bypass the nourishment that would give us succor. We miss the quiet that would give us wisdom. We miss the joy and love born of effortless delight. Poisoned by this hypnotic belief that good things come only through unceasing determination and tireless effort, we can never truly rest. And for want of rest, our lives are in danger.

In our drive for success we are seduced by the promises of more: more money, more recognition, more satisfaction, more love, more information, more influence, more possessions, more security. Even when our intentions are noble and our efforts sincere—even when we dedicate our lives to the service of others—the corrosive pressure of frantic overactivity can nonetheless cause suffering in ourselves and others.

A "successful" life has become a violent enterprise. We make war on our own bodies, pushing them beyond their limits; war on our children, because we cannot find enough time to be with them when they are hurt and afraid, and need our company; war on our spirit, because we are too preoccupied to listen to the quiet voices that seek to nourish and refresh us; war on our communities, because we are fearfully protecting what we have, and do not feel safe enough to be kind and generous; war on the earth, because we cannot take the time to place our feet on the ground and allow it to feed us, to taste its blessings and give thanks.

As the founder of a public charity, I visit the large offices of wealthy donors, the crowded rooms of social service agencies, and the small houses of the poorest families. Remarkably, within this mosaic there is a universal refrain: *I am so busy*. It does not seem to matter if the people I speak with are doctors or day-care workers, shopkeepers or social workers, parents or teachers, nurses or lawyers, students or therapists, community activists or cooks.

Whether they are Hispanic or Native American, Caucasian or Black, the more their lives speed up, the more they feel hurt, frightened, and isolated. Despite their good hearts and equally good intentions, their work in the world rarely feels light, pleasant, or healing. Instead, as it all piles endlessly upon itself, the whole experience of being alive begins to melt into one enormous obligation. It becomes the standard greeting everywhere: *I am so busy*.

We say this to one another with no small degree of pride, as if our exhaustion were a trophy, our ability to withstand stress a mark of real character. The busier we are, the more important we seem to ourselves and, we imagine, to others. To be unavailable to our friends and family, to be unable to find time for the sunset (or even to know that the sun has set at all), to whiz through our obligations without time for a single, mindful breath, this has become the model of a successful life.

Our lack of rest and reflection is not just a personal affliction. It colors the way we build and sustain community, it dictates the way we respond to suffering, and it shapes the ways in which we seek peace and healing in the world. I have worked for twenty-five years in the fields of community development, public health, mental health, and criminal justice. With a few notable exceptions, the way problems are solved is frantically, desperately, reactively, and badly. Despite their well-meaning and generous souls, community and corporate leaders are infected with a fearful desperation that is corrosive to genuine helpfulness, justice, or healing. As Brother David Steindl-Rast reminds us, the Chinese pictograph for "busy" is composed of two characters: *heart* and *killing*.

THOMAS MERTON:

There is a pervasive form of contemporary violence . . . [and that is] activism and overwork. The rush and pressure of modern life are a form, perhaps the most common form, of its innate violence.

To allow oneself to be carried away by a multitude of conflicting concerns, to surrender to too many demands, to commit oneself to too many projects, to want to help everyone in everything, is to succumb to violence.

The frenzy of our activism neutralizes our work for peace. It destroys our own inner capacity for peace. It destroys the fruitfulness of our own work, because it kills the root of inner wisdom which makes work fruitful.

Harvard president Neil Rudenstine overslept one morning in November 1994. For this zealous perfectionist, in the midst of a million-dollar-a-day fund-raising campaign, it was cause for alarm. After years of intensive, nonstop toil and struggle in an atmosphere that rewarded frantic busyness and over-work, and having been assaulted by a hail of never-finished tasks, President Rudenstine collapsed. "My sense was that I was exhausted," Rudenstine told reporters. His doctor agreed. Only after a three-month sabbatical, during which he read Lewis Thomas, listened to Ravel, and walked with his wife on a Caribbean beach, was Rudenstine able to return to his post. That week, his picture was on the cover of *Newsweek* magazine beside the one-word banner headline: "Exhausted!"

I have sat on dozens of boards and commissions with many fine, compassionate, and generous people who are so tired, overwhelmed, and overworked that they have neither the time nor the capacity to listen to the deeper voices that speak to the essence of the problems before them. Presented with the intricate and delicate issues of poverty, public health, community well-being, and crime, our impulse, born of wea-riness, is to rush headlong toward doing anything that will make the problem go away. Maybe then we can finally go home and get some rest. But without the essential nutrients of rest, wisdom, and delight embedded in the problem-solving process itself, the solution we patch together is likely to be an obstacle to genuine relief. Born of desperation, it often con-tains enough fundamental inaccuracy to guarantee an equally perplexing problem will emerge as soon as it is put into place. In the soil of the quick fix is the seed of a new problem, because our quiet wisdom is unavailable.

What makes life fruitful? The attainment of wisdom? The establishment of a just and fair society? The creation of beauty? The practice of loving-kindness? Thomas Jefferson suggested that human life and liberty were intimately en-twined with the pursuit of happiness. Instead, life has become a maelstrom in which speed and accomplishment, consump-tion and productivity have become the most valued human commodities. In the trance of overwork, we take everything for granted. We consume things, people, and information. We do not have time to savor this life, nor to care deeply and gently for ourselves, our loved ones, or our world; rather, with increasingly dizzying haste, we use them all up, and throw them away. Can this be the happiness of which Jefferson spoke?

How have we allowed this to happen? This was not our intention, this is not the world we dreamed when we were young and our whole life was full of possibility and promise. How did we get so terribly lost in a world saturated with striving and grasping, yet somehow bereft of joy and delight?

I suggest that it is this: We have forgotten the Sabbath.

Before you dismiss this statement as simplistic, even naive, we must explore more fully the nature and definition of Sabbath. While Sabbath can refer to a single day of the week, Sabbath can also be a far-reaching, revolutionary tool for cultivating those precious human qualities that grow only in time.

If busyness can become a kind of violence, we do not have to stretch our perception very far to see that Sabbath time—effortless, nourishing rest—can invite a healing of this violence. When we consecrate a time to listen to the still, small voices, we remember the root of inner wisdom that makes work fruitful. We remember from where we are most deeply nourished, and see more clearly the shape and texture of the people and things before us.

Without rest, we respond from a survival mode, where everything we meet assumes a terrifying prominence. When we are driving a motorcycle at high speed, even a small stone in the road can be a deadly threat. So, when we are moving faster and faster, every encounter, every detail inflates in importance, everything seems more urgent than it really is, and we react with sloppy desperation.

Charles is a gifted, thoughtful physician. One day we were discussing the effects of exhaustion on the quality of our work. Physicians are trained to work when they are exhausted, required from the moment they begin medical school to perform when they are sleep-deprived, hurried, and over-loaded. "I discovered in medical school," Charles told me, "that if I saw a patient when I was tired or overworked, I would order a lot of tests. I was so exhausted, I couldn't tell exactly what was going on. I could see the symptoms, I could recognize the possible diagnoses, but I couldn't really hear how it all fit together. So I got in the habit of ordering a battery of tests, hoping they would tell me what I was missing.

"But when I was rested—if I had an opportunity to get some sleep, or go for a quiet walk—when I saw the next patient, I could rely on my intuition and experience to give me a pretty accurate reading of what was happening. If there was any uncertainty about my diagnosis, I would order a single, specific test to confirm or deny it. But when I could take the time to listen and be present with them and their illness, I was almost always right."

Sabbath time can be a revolutionary challenge to the violence of overwork, mindless accumulation, and the endless multiplication of desires, responsibilities, and accomplishments. Sabbath is a way of being in time where we remember who we are, remember what we know, and taste the gifts of spirit and eternity.

Like a path through the forest, Sabbath creates a marker for ourselves so, if we are lost, we can find our way back to our center. "Remember the Sabbath" means "Remember that everything you have received is a blessing. Remember to delight in your life, in the fruits of your labor. Remember to stop and offer thanks for the wonder of it." *Remember*, as if we would forget. Indeed, the assumption is that we will forget. And history has proven that, given enough time, we will.

"Remember the Sabbath" is not simply a life-style suggestion. It is a spiritual precept in most of the world's spiritual traditions—ethical precepts that include prohibitions against killing, stealing, and lying. How can forgetting the Sabbath possibly be morally and socially dangerous? How can forgetting to be restful, sing songs, and take delight in creation be as reprehensible as murder, robbery, and deceit? Why is this so important?

Sabbath honors the necessary wisdom of dormancy. If certain plant species, for example, do not lie dormant for winter, they will not bear fruit in the spring. If this continues for more than a season, the plant begins to die. If dormancy continues to be prevented, the entire species will die. A period of rest—in which nutrition and fertility most readily coalesce—is not simply a human psychological convenience; it is a spiritual and biological necessity. A lack of dormancy produces confusion and erosion in the life force.

We, too, must have a period in which we lie fallow, and restore our souls. In Sabbath time we remember to celebrate what is beautiful and sacred; we light candles, sing songs, tell stories, eat, nap, and make love. It is a time to let our work, our lands, our animals lie fallow, to be nourished and refreshed. Within this sanctuary, we become available to the insights and blessings of deep mindfulness that arise only in stillness and time. When we act from a place of deep rest, we are more capable of cultivating what the Buddhists would call right understanding, right action, and right effort. In a complex and unstable world, if we do not rest, if we do not surrender into some kind of Sabbath, how can we find our way, how can we hear the voices that tell us the right thing to do?

Throughout this book I use the word *Sabbath* both as a specific practice and a larger metaphor, a starting point to invoke a conversation about the forgotten necessity of rest. Sabbath is time for sacred rest; it may be a holy day, the seventh day of the week, as in the Jewish tradition, or the first day of the week, as for Christians. But Sabbath time may also be a Sabbath afternoon, a Sabbath hour, a Sabbath walk—indeed, anything that preserves a visceral experience of life-giving nourishment and rest. I have included dozens of Sabbath exercises, simple practices that can take a few hours or a few moments. Sabbath time is time off the wheel, time when we take our hand from the plow and let God and the earth care for things, while we drink, if only for a few moments, from the fountain of rest and delight.

Sabbath is more than the absence of work; it is not just a day off, when we catch up on television or errands. It is the presence of something that arises when we consecrate a period of time to listen to what is most deeply beautiful, nourishing, or true. It is time consecrated with our attention, our mindfulness, honoring those quiet forces of grace or spirit that sustain and heal us.

I invoke the Sabbath for its proven wisdom over the ages. But I also call on the authority that still clings to its name. While many of us are terribly weary, we have come to associate tremendous guilt and shame with taking time to rest. Sabbath gives us permission; it commands us to stop. As part of the Judeo-Christian tradition, it is already woven into the fabric of our society. Many can still recall when, not long ago, shops and stores were closed on Sundays. Those quiet Sunday afternoons are embedded in our cultural memory, even if they are no longer practiced.

Sabbath does not require us to leave home, change jobs, go on retreat, or leave the world of ordinary life. We do not have to change clothes or purchase any expensive spiritual equipment. We only need to remember.

Sabbath time is not spiritually superior to our work. The practice is rather to find that balance point at which, having rested, we do our work with greater ease and joy, and bring healing and delight to our endeavors. Even if we were to leave work behind and seek the comfort and security of a monastery, we would be handed a broom, and told to sweep the walks. Even in monasteries we must cook and clean, build and repair, garden and sweep. But there is a time to sweep, and a time to put down the broom and rest.

When the Mass begins in a cathedral, the space is transformed the instant the first prayer is offered. The space is not different, but the time has been transformed.

When monks enter an ashram or monastery and sit in silence, only when the bell is rung does the meditation begin. The space may be the same, but the time is consecrated by the mindfulness that arises in the striking of the bell.

When Muslims are called to prayer five times each day, all work ceases, and all the ancient words, spoken aloud for centuries, rise like fragrance to the skies.

Just so, during Sabbath the Jews, by keeping sacred rest, could maintain their spiritual ground wherever they were, even in protracted exile from their own country. *It was not Israel that kept the Sabbath*, it is said, *but the Sabbath kept Israel.*

The practice of Sabbath is like the practice of taking refuge. In Buddhism, one takes refuge in the Buddha nature, and in the wisdom of the Buddha and in the family of the Buddha. In so doing, we join the company of all those who have sought healing and liberation, we surrender into that place where Buddha-nature already lives within us, and we align our intention with our innate, natural perfection. Thus, when we sit in meditation, all the saints and ancestors send us loving-kindness, as they accompany our each and every breath.

Jesus offered this same beautiful practice to his disciples. *Make your home in me*, he said, *as I make mine in you.* The kingdom is within you, he reminded them, alive and miraculous this very moment. I am with you always: When you come to rest, you will feel me. You will remember who you are, that you are the light of the world.

Much of modern life, of course, is specifically designed to seduce our attention away from this inner place of refuge. When we are in the world with eyes wide open, the seductions are insatiable. Hundreds of channels of cable and satellite television; telephones with multiple lines and call-waiting, so we can talk to more than one person at a time; fax machines; mail, e-mail, and overnight mail; billboards; magazines; newspapers; radio. Every stimulus competes for our attention: Buy me. Do me. Watch me. Try me. Drink me. It is as if we have inadvertently stumbled into some horrific wonderland.

Sabbath time can become our refuge. During the Sabbath, we set aside a sanctuary in time, disconnect from the frenzy of consumption and accomplishment, and consecrate our day as an offering for healing all beings.

This book is, then, a plea for Sabbath-keeping. In part for ourselves, in part so that when we go forth to heal the wounds of our world, whatever we build, create, craft, or serve will have the wisdom of rest in it.

Ten years ago a group of friends and I founded Bread for the Journey—a small, nonprofit charity—to serve the needs of people and communities. Listening closely to people who live in impoverished neighborhoods, we uncover those quiet saints who seek to serve their communities. Our work is simply to find them, and help their work come to fruition. While they have very little money, they are rich in other things far more valuable—wisdom and courage, passion and faith. With a little support from Bread for the Journey, their time, energy, and commitment blossom into day-care centers, food banks, youth programs, community centers, mentoring programs.

Our work is fruitful only when we are quiet enough to

hear the miraculous resilience and strength present among those who suffer, patient enough to see the light that shines in the midst of darkness. Thus, Sabbath is not only for ourselves; rested and refreshed, we more generously serve all those who need our care. The human spirit is naturally generous; the instant we are filled, our first impulse is to be useful, to be kind, to give something away.

In the past few years a quiet, growing network of people have contacted us, wanting to start Bread for the Journey chapters across the country. Once people feel nourished and refreshed, they cannot help but be kind; just so, the world aches for the generosity of a well-rested people.

So let us remember the Sabbath. Let us breathe deeply in the rhythms of life, of the earth, of action and rest. Traditionally, Sabbath is honored by lighting candles, gathering in worship and prayer, blessing children, singing songs, keeping silence, walking, reading scripture, making love, sharing a meal. Just as we must wait until the darkness falls before we can see the stars, so does the Sabbath quietly wait for us. As darkness falls, as the light of the world fades and disappears, we light the inner lights, the lights of home and refuge. Our steps take us home, and the light draws us in.

May you find some comfort here.

A Note on the Exercises

I have included stories, poems, and practices at the end of each chapter. You may explore a Sabbath practice for yourself by trying a few and, as time goes on, weaving several together into a Sabbath morning, afternoon, or entire day.

Because the Jewish Sabbath is so richly evolved, containing a vast wealth of history and ritual, I often use the Jewish Sabbath as a starting point. However, I am not Jewish—a fact that Zalman Schachter-Shalomi, the respected rabbi and scholar, noted when he gleefully introduced me at the Naropa Institute as "the *goy* who loves Shabbos."

I have therefore tried to offer a rich mixture of practices from various traditions, including my own Christian tradition. Some form of Sabbath time is practiced by Jews and Christians, by Buddhists and Muslims, Hindus and native tribes around the world. You may find a deep ache to gather with others in worship at church, synagogue, or in meditation; at other times you may feel pulled toward home, friends, or solitude. Please use these practices to find a Sabbath rest that most fruitfully nourishes your heart and body.

The chapters and exercises have their own inner rhythm. Feel free to play with, modify, edit, expand, or ignore whatever you like. I only hope you will find in these pages some taste of Sabbath delight.

LET EVENING COME

Let the light of late afternoon
shine through chinks in the barn, moving
up the bales as the sun moves down.

Let the cricket take up chafing
as a woman takes up her needles
and her yarn. Let evening come.

Let dew collect on the hoe abandoned
in long grass. Let the stars appear
and the moon disclose her silver horn.

Let the fox go back to its sandy den.
Let the wind die down. Let the shed
go black inside. Let evening come.

To the bottle in the ditch, to the scoop
in the oats, to the air in the lung
let evening come.

Let it come as it will, and don't
be afraid. God does not leave us
comfortless, so let evening come.

—JANE KENYON

REST

REST FOR THE WEARY

There is more to life
than merely increasing its speed.
— GANDHI

September. I am surrounded by flowers. Every day more flowers, until I beg the nurses to share them with other patients who could be cheered by them. A colleague from the AIDS clinic drops by to sing "The Lord's Prayer" in a rich alto at my feet. One visitor, a former client, brings me a tiny Buddha. An old friend brings me my favorite chicken enchiladas with green chili. Another sits beside me and, using a Tibetan practice, breathes in my suffering while he breathes out healing and strength for me. A neighbor brings me a picture of Our Lady of Guadalupe. My son brings me Gizmo, his favorite stuffed animal, to watch over me in the night. Many come, I find out later, and depart without waking me. I have no idea who came and who did not. I am exhausted. I cannot lift my head or open my eyes.

I am close to death, infected with streptococcal pneumonia, a rare and often fatal bacterial infection. Jim Henson, the inventive puppeteer, died from this illness. I breathe only with great difficulty. I am on an emergency schedule: Every four hours, someone comes and gives me albuterol to inhale. Then I am tilted upside down by a respiratory therapist, who pummels me on my back and sides while I lie with my head below my feet. They are trying to make me cough up the phlegm that is choking me to death.

A month earlier, I had been living a typical life, at least for me. I was seeing patients in psychotherapy, running Bread for the Journey, and traveling around the country, lecturing and teaching. When I was at home I served as the chaplain in the AIDS clinic in Santa Fe, and I was also finishing a book while trying my best to be a good husband and father. A month earlier, I had put a quote from Brother David Steindl-Rast on my bulletin board. Life, he said, was like the breath: We must be able to live in an easy rhythm between give and take. If we cannot learn to live and breathe in this rhythm, he counseled, we will place ourselves in grave danger.

Here I am, exhausted, barely able to breathe at all. I am attached and entwined; long plastic tubes feed me nourishing fluids, antibiotics, oxygen. Visitors, each bringing their particular gift of kindness, both comfort and tire me. Even with dear friends I feel the energy go out of me, the energy of attention, of listening to words, of being even marginally present. At the end of each visit, I fall immediately back to sleep before my visitors are out the door.

I had always assumed that people I loved gave energy to me, and people I disliked took it away from me. Now I see that every act, no matter how pleasant or nourishing, requires effort, consumes oxygen. Every gesture, every thought or touch, uses some life.

I am reminded of the story of Jesus walking through a crowd of people. A woman, seeking to be healed, reached out to touch the hem of his garment. Jesus asked, *Who touched me?* His disciples said, *People are touching you all the time, what are you talking about?* But Jesus said, *I could feel power go out of me.* Deeply mindful of the flow of his life force, Jesus could feel the expenditure of energy in every encounter.

This is a useful discovery for how our days go. We meet dozens of people, have so many conversations. We do not feel how much energy we spend on each activity, because we imagine we will always have more energy at our disposal. This one little conversation, this one extra phone call, this one quick meeting, what can it cost? But it does cost, it drains yet another drop of our life. Then, at the end of days, weeks, months, years, we collapse, we burn out, and cannot see where it happened. It happened in a thousand unconscious events, tasks, and responsibilities that seemed easy and harmless on the surface but that each, one after the other, used a small portion of our precious life.

And so we are given a commandment: Remember the Sabbath. Rest is an essential enzyme of life, as necessary as air. Without rest, we cannot sustain the energy needed to have life. We refuse to rest at our peril—and yet in a world where overwork is seen as a professional virtue, many of us feel we can legitimately be stopped only by physical illness or collapse.

My friend Will is a gifted physician who was always busy. When Will barely survived a massive heart attack, he used his illness as an opportunity to reevaluate his life, and began to slow down, taking particular care to take time with his grandchildren. Helena is a passionate and driven massage therapist who found a lump in her breast and, upon discovering it was cancer, began to paint, do yoga, and nap in her hammock in the afternoons. Pamela, an overworked social worker, was nearly killed in a hit-and-run collision, and during her long rehabilitation she began to listen carefully for those things that brought her nourishment and joy. She remembered times of prayer and worship as a child, and felt comforted by the fragrance of her early spirituality. When she recovered sufficiently, she entered the seminary and became a pastoral counselor. She now serves those in need with gentle enthusiasm. Dolores was a devoted psychotherapist with a thriving private practice with far more clients than she could realistically serve. She was felled by a mysterious illness that left her weak and physically exhausted for almost three years. Later, with fewer clients, and the fragrance of rest in her body, her ears and eyes have become like crystal; she hears and sees deeply into the hearts of those who come to her.

If we do not allow for a rhythm of rest in our overly busy lives, illness becomes our Sabbath—our pneumonia, our cancer, our heart attack, our accidents create Sabbath for us. In my relationships with people suffering with cancer, AIDS, and other life-threatening illness, I am always struck by the mixture of sadness and relief they experience when illness interrupts their overly busy lives. While each shares their particular fears and sorrows, almost every one confesses some secret gratefulness. "Finally," they say, "at last. I can rest."

Through a good friend and doctor who literally threw me into his pickup truck and raced me to the hospital, through the wise and swift administration of good medicine, through numberless prayers and great kindnesses, I was granted the blessing of being healed of my infection. Now, I take more walks. I play with my children, I work mostly with the poor, and have stopped seeing patients. I write when I am able, and I pray more. I try to be kind. And without fail, at the close of the day, I stop, say a prayer, and give thanks. The greatest lesson I have learned is about surrender. There are larger forces, strong and wise, at work here. I am willing to be stopped. I owe my life to the simple act of rest.

Lighting Sabbath Candles

The traditional Jewish Sabbath begins at sundown, the Christian Sabbath with morning worship. In both, Sabbath time begins with the lighting of candles. Those who celebrate Sabbath find that in this moment, the stopping truly begins. They take a few breaths, allow the mind to quiet, and the quality of the day begins to shift. Irene says she can feel the tension leave her body as the wick takes the flame. Kathy says she often weeps, so great is her relief that the time for rest has come. This is the beginning of sacred time.

Even Sara, who does not celebrate Sabbath at all, tells me that when she has prepared dinner for her family and is ready to eat, she is especially fond of the moment she lights the candles. It is, she says, a kind of silent grace, a ritual beginning of family time.

WILL

Three generations back
my family had only

to light a candle
and the world parted.

Today, Friday afternoon,
I disconnect clocks and phones.

When night fills my house
with passages,

I begin saving
my life.

— MARCIA FALK

Find a candle that holds some beauty or meaning for you. When you have set aside some time—before a meal, or during prayer, meditation, or simply quiet reading—set the candle before you, say a simple prayer or blessing for yourself or someone you love, and light the candle. Take a few mindful breaths. For just this moment, let the hurry of the world fall away.

THE JOY OF REST

Better is one hand full of quietness
than two hands full of toil
and a striving after wind.
— ECCLESIASTES 4:6

When I gather with friends and colleagues for Sabbath retreats, those courageous few who manage to carve out a day or a weekend for quiet reflection often arrive thoroughly exhausted. By the afternoon, some inevitably fall asleep right in the middle of our meditations. When they awaken they quickly apologize for their spiritual transgressions; they feel ashamed and embarrassed. I reassure them it is good when they sleep. It is a sign of trust, that they feel safe enough finally to let go and surrender to their weariness.

And what a great weariness it is. Most of us do not

realize how tired we really are until we go away on vacation or retreat, and cannot even keep our eyes open.

Jacqueline comes to a retreat directly from work. She has an important position in the state legislature. As an aide to a legislative leader, she is always at the center of great frantic activity. She writes bills, lobbies legislators, meets with constituents, soothes egos, puts out fires, and quells the inevitable flaring angers and frustrations that saturate the legislative morass. She is skillful and kind, and respected by her peers. Still, when she is finally able to leave work, often at a late hour, she tends to her three children with a mixture of weariness, need, and guilt. When she arrives at our retreat, she feels drained and depleted. "I am so tired," she says. "I am with people all day and night, but I still feel so lonely. My soul feels dry. Even when things work well, when I can break away from work and spend some time with my kids, nothing seems to heal this fatigue, this sense of guilt and duty and responsibility. It all feels so heavy." Jacqueline sits back and quietly weeps.

When Moses becomes weary, leading his people through their trials in the desert, God tells him, *My presence will go with you, and I will give you rest.* Jesus tells his disciples, *Come to me all who toil and are heavy laden, and I will give you rest.* For Moses as for Jesus, rest is a precious ointment, a balm for the heavy heart. Jesus, for whom anything was possible, did not offer "seven secret coping strategies" to get work done faster, or "nine spiritual stress management techniques" to enhance our effectiveness. Instead, he offered the simple practice of rest as a natural, nourishing, and essential companion to our work. *Learn from me,* he invited, *and you will find rest for your souls.*

When we think of Jesus, we usually think of him teaching, healing, or being accosted by the hordes of sick or possessed who sought his touch. But Jesus would just as often send people away, or disappear without warning, dismissing those in need with neither excuse nor explanation, and retreat to a place of rest.

And after he had dismissed the crowds, he went up on the mountain by himself to pray. When evening came, he was there alone. (MATTHEW 14:23)

But so much the more the report went abroad concerning him; and great multitudes gathered to hear and to be healed of their infirmities. But he withdrew into the wilderness and prayed. (LUKE 5:15–16)

That evening, at sundown, they brought to him all who were sick or possessed with demons. And the whole city was gathered together about the door . . . And in the morning, a great while before the day, he rose and went out to a lonely place, and there he prayed. And Simon and those who were with him pursued him. (MARK 1:32–33, 35–36)

Jesus did not wait until everyone had been properly cared for, until all who sought him were healed. He did not ask permission to go, nor did he leave anyone behind "on call," or even let his disciples know where he was going. Jesus obeyed a deeper rhythm. When the moment for rest had come, the time for healing was over. He would simply stop, retire to a quiet place, and pray.

Sometimes he would take the disciples with him—*Come away to a deserted place all by yourselves and rest for a while,* he would tell them. He did not wait until they had completed all their work; he invited them to rest in the middle of their busyness, when they had no leisure, even to eat. *Come with me,* he said. *Let us go, and rest, and pray.*

One translation of the biblical phrase "to pray" is "to come to rest." When Jesus prayed he was at rest, nourished by the healing spirit that saturates those still, quiet places. In the Jesus tradition, prayer can be a practice of simply being in the presence of God, allowing the mind to rest in the heart. This can help us begin to understand one aspect of Sabbath time: a period of repose, when the mind settles gently in the heart.

Who is it that can make muddy water clear? asks the Tao Te Ching. *But if allowed to remain still, it will gradually become clear of itself.* The invitation to rest is rooted in an undeniable spiritual gravity that allows all things at rest to settle, to find their place. There comes a moment in our striving when more effort actually becomes counterproductive, when our frantic busyness only muddies the waters of our wisdom and understanding. When we become still and allow our life to rest, we feel a renewal of energy and gradual clarity of perception. The Psalmist speaks of this: *He makes me lie down in green pastures; He leads me beside still waters. He restores my soul.* Here we have another stunning principle undergirding Sabbath time: God does not want us to be exhausted. God wants us to be happy.

The practice of Shabbat, or Sabbath, is designed specifically to restore us, a gift of time in which we allow the cares and concerns of the marketplace to fall away. We set aside time to delight in being alive, to savor the gifts of creation, and to give thanks for the blessings we may have missed in our necessary preoccupation with our work. Ancient texts suggest we light candles, sing songs, pray, tell stories, worship, eat, nap, and make love. It is a day of delight, a sanctuary in time. Within this sanctuary, we make ourselves available to the insights and blessings that arise only in stillness and time.

Creating Time and Space

My friend Jacob told me this story. "When Sheila and I were married, her grandparents gave us a brand-new washer and dryer. It was a very generous gift, and we were very grateful to receive such a blessing for our new home. But when they presented them to us, her grandfather explained that this was a Jewish washer and dryer. 'What makes them Jewish?' I asked, naively. Sheila's grandfather replied with a twinkle, 'They won't work on Shabbat.'"

Dorothy works for a pharmaceutical company. While she will work long and hard during the week, often staying late or working extra hours, she always leaves work at five on Friday, no matter what. She has arranged it with her employer that she will be efficient and devoted while there, but will be completely finished and gone by five. Then she goes home to her husband; their children are grown, and so they share a quiet, intimate meal, and begin their Sabbath weekend—usually a mixture of reading, retreat, walking, and time with friends.

Sabbath can only begin if we close the factory, turn out the lights, turn off the computer, and withdraw from the concerns of the marketplace. Choose at least one heavily used appliance or device—the telephone, television, computer, washer and dryer—and let them rest for a Sabbath period. Whether it is a morning, afternoon, or entire day, surrender to a quality of time when you will not be disturbed, seduced, or responsive to

what our technologies have to offer. Notice how you respond to
its absence.

> What I want is to leap out of this personality
> And then sit apart from that leaping—
> I've lived too long where I can be reached.

— RUMI

LEGALISM AND THE
DREARY SABBATH

You are not made for the Sabbath;
the Sabbath is made for you.

— MARK 2:27

On the seventh day, God rests. Jewish texts prohibit thirty-nine specific acts during Sabbath—acts traditionally associated with the rebuilding of the temple in Jerusalem. If God could rest in creating the universe, God's people could rest in the building of the sacred temple. Tasks such as sowing, plowing, reaping, threshing, and winnowing are prohibited, as are grinding, sifting, kneading, and baking. Spinning and weaving, hunting and slaughtering, building, hammering, and transporting are among the prohibitions. But beyond the legalism is an idea that by saying no to making some things happen, deep permission arises for other things to happen. When we cease our daily labor, other things—love, friendship, prayer, touch, singing, rest—can be born in the space created by our rest. Walking with a friend, reciting a prayer, caring for children, sharing bread and wine with family and neighbors—those are intimate graces that need precious time and attention.

Over time, as with all ecclesiastical precepts, Sabbath laws became overly legalistic. The Jewish Sabbath could be so restrictive and morose that, for some, it became a day of lethargy and depression rather than sensuality and delight. Laughter, play, even walks in nature were at one point forbidden. Zalman Schachter-Shalomi told me, "Lots of people will swear allegiance to the Sabbath and criticize those who do not keep all the Sabbath laws. But their inner experience is not one of spaciousness and delight. It is too easy to talk of prohibition, but the point is the space and time created to say yes to sacred spirituality, sensuality, sexuality, prayer, rest, song, delight. It is not about legalism and legislation, but about joy and the things that grow only in time. We need to remove the grimness from it." As a beginning, Reb Zalman suggests we begin the Sabbath simply by saying, "Today I am going to pamper my soul."

Early Christians celebrated the Sabbath on Sunday, to commemorate the day of Jesus' resurrection. The Sunday Sabbath first received official recognition in 321 C.E., when the emperor Constantine, newly converted to Christianity, declared it a day of rest throughout the Roman Empire. Sadly, this inaugurated a long period of governmentally enforced Sabbath-keeping, when church attendance became mandatory. Much later, when religious reform swept through Europe in the sixteenth century, it brought renewed emphasis on long, arduous worship services, designed in part to steer the faithful away from the more sensual temptations of a day of rest. As church fever spread throughout the New World, American Protestantism increased the severity and duration of Sabbath obligations as further evidence of a deeper piety. Small wonder, then, that so many of us chafe at the memory of such stringent Sabbath restrictions, and actually prefer to work rather than be forced to rest in such a dry and gloomy fashion.

Sarah was raised by her Jewish grandparents. She remembers the Sabbath as a day on which she couldn't turn on any lights, see her friends, or go outside and play. On the Sabbath she felt trapped in a dreary world that felt dark and punitive. David, raised in a strict Christian household, recalls Sundays as being similarly bleak. "We were not allowed to do anything fun—no games, no card playing, not even baseball. All we could do was sit inside, usually with my grandparents, and eat, and talk, or just do nothing."

Reb Zalman says the people who wrote such restrictive laws were undoubtedly people who "completely missed the joy of the Sabbath." The ancient Jewish *Mekilta* teaches "The Sabbath is given unto you, not you unto the Sabbath." Jesus similarly insisted that "Man is not made for the Sabbath, but Sabbath is made for man." These teachings clearly warn against the tendency toward legalism, which suffocates our joy, and drains the spontaneity and passion out of this gratuitous day of delight.

Among the many Sabbath practitioners who have shared their stories with me, one of the more popular Sabbath activities is making love. Indeed, the Talmud tractate on marriage contracts states that the righteous couple should make love every Friday night. One practitioner told me that it is traditional among some sects to make love four times during the Sabbath. Hearing this, I respectfully inquired as to whether he and his wife did, in fact, faithfully keep this particular precept. "No, we make love only once. But," he added with a twinkle, "we hold a deep intention for the other three."

The God who made the Sabbath is not a cranky schoolmaster, always forbidding, coercing obedience, and watching sniveling subjects slinking about in cowardly compliance. The Sabbath commandment comes from a kind, wise teacher who does not like to see us suffer. Let me make it easier for you,

God says. Some things at first may seem expedient, or important, or profitable—but in the end, they will bring you suffering. If you work all week and forget to rest, you will become brittle and hard, and lose precious nourishment and joy. Forgetting the Sabbath is like forgetting to unwrap the most beautiful gift under the tree.

If we forget to rest we will work too hard and forget our more tender mercies, forget those we love, forget our children and our natural wonder. God says: Please, don't. It is a waste of a tremendous gift I have given you. If you knew the value of your life, you would not waste a single breath. So I give you this commandment: Remember to rest. This is not a lifestyle suggestion, but a commandment—as important as not stealing, not murdering, or not lying. Remember to play and bless and make love and eat with those you love, and take comfort, easy and long, in this gift of sacred rest.

> If you . . . call the Sabbath a delight . . .
> then you shall take delight in the Lord,
> and I will make you ride upon the
> heights of the earth.

> —ISAIAH 58:13–14

A Sabbath Meal

A simple way to begin Sabbath time is with a meal, alone or shared with those we love. One of my favorite meals was always the one we shared after church on Sundays when I was in college. A good friend had been ordained as a Presbyterian minister, and a dozen of us would tumble into her house after church, put on some rock and roll, make sandwiches, pile up snacks and drinks, and eat around a big table. We ate and talked and laughed and played all day long into night. It was my first real introduction to a joyful Sabbath.

Julie is a secretary in a big city. She lives in an apartment, and misses the country. "I started walking to a market downtown every week to get fresh flowers, and a few times a week to make a Sabbath meal, to grind the spices by hand, separate the beans, wash the vegetables. As easy as it is in the city to get food already prepared, I chose to make a few meals by hand, often inviting friends to join me. It is time away from work and responsibility. It becomes almost sacred, sacramental, the way food and hands and friendship all work together in the warmth of the kitchen."

Prepare a Sabbath meal, alone or with friends or family. Shop for the ingredients, choosing those that bring you the most pleasure. This food is not so much for survival as for sheer, savory delight. Put on some music, turn off the phone. Take as much time as you like to feel, taste, smell each ingredient, every spice, bread, and vegetable. Decorate the table with flowers, colorful placemats, and candles. Say a prayer. Give thanks, remembering all the people who grew, harvested, packed, shipped, and sold them for you. Give thanks for the bounty of the earth. Enjoy.

A NEW BEGINNING

> In the beginning God created the heavens
> and the earth. The earth was without form
> and void, and darkness was upon
> the face of the deep; and the Spirit of God
> was moving over the face of the waters.
>
> — GENESIS 1:1–2

Sabbath time is first revealed in the Genesis creation story, a tale that boldly reveals the stuff the world is made of. It begins with emptiness, a great void out of which emerges all life.

In the beginning, the spirit-wind of God moves across the face of the deep. The deep is not barren but pregnant, an emptiness teeming with the promise of life. Rabbi Zalman Schachter-Shalomi suggests a more accurate reading of the Hebrew would be "In *a* beginning," as if there were endless beginnings in the cycle of life. Biblical scholars also agree that the phrase

"God created" would be better translated "when God *began to create*." So the story literally begins: *In a beginning, when God began to create the heavens and the earth . . .*

Creation, then, is an ongoing story of new beginnings, opportunities to begin again and again. God began to create, is still creating; nothing is finished. Creation continues to arise out of emptiness, take form, and dissolve over time, dust to dust, returning to emptiness. All life arises and falls away in this beautiful, fruitful rhythm.

Later, in the book of Exodus, we read, "In six days God made heaven and earth, and on the seventh day God rested, and was refreshed." Here, the word "refreshed," *vaiynafesh,* literally means, *and God exhaled.* The creation of the world was like the life-quickening inhale; the Sabbath is the exhale. Thus, in a beginning, all creation moves with the rhythm of the inhale and the exhale. Without the Sabbath exhale, the life-giving inhale is impossible.

Most spiritual traditions celebrate some form of Sabbath practice. Before the Hebrews, the Babylonians celebrated a lunar Sabbath, also a day of rest. Buddhists use a lunar Sabbath—on the new, full, and quarter moons—as a day for monks and lay people to feast together, meditate, reflect on the dharma, and recite the fundamental precepts of spiritual practice. Christians and Muslims celebrate their Sabbath days on Sunday and Friday respectively, both using sacred time to regularly focus their heart's attention on spiritual matters, and to gather together, celebrate their love for one another, and take delight in beginning together anew.

The Jewish Sabbath became crucial when the Temple in Jerusalem was destroyed in 70 C.E. When the Jews were in exile, the Sabbath became their temple, their sanctuary in time. It traveled with them wherever they went, a movable feast, a holy of holies that faithfully accompanied them in adversity. The practice of Sabbath was a spiritual glue that held the people together. This is perhaps one reason why the Sabbath commandment is the one most discussed and reiterated throughout the Torah.

It is not surprising that the Dalai Lama, concerned about the preservation of Tibetan spiritual life in exile, recently sought advice from a gathering of rabbis and other Jewish scholars on those observances—such as Sabbath, Passover, Hanukkah, other home-based spiritual practices—that so faithfully sustained the Jews through centuries of exile. It seemed crucial for the Dalai Lama to understand how a sanctuary not dependent upon a geographic place but consecrated in holy time, available to everyone, in every place—like the practice of Sabbath—could help cultivate and maintain the spiritual heart of the Tibetan people as they suffer their own modern-day exile from the temple of their homeland.

There is yet one more aspect of the Sabbath that I find particularly delicious. God creates the world in six days, and on the seventh day, God rests. But a closer reading of Genesis reveals that the Sabbath was not simply a day off. It says, "On the seventh day God finished God's work." How can this be? Wasn't the seventh day when God, exhausted, took time off and rested, satisfied with the laborious work of creation?

The ancient rabbis teach that on the seventh day, God created *menuha*—tranquillity, serenity, peace, and repose—rest, in the deepest possible sense of fertile, healing stillness. Until the Sabbath, creation was unfinished. Only after the birth of *menuha,* only with tranquillity and rest, was the circle of creation made full and complete.

Christians celebrate Sabbath at the beginning of the week, to commemorate Jesus' resurrection. We remember the tender gratefulness of Mary, who went out in the early morning to weep for a beloved friend who had died—only to hear his loving voice comfort and caress her. Sabbath implies a willingness to be surprised by unexpected grace, to partake of those potent moments when creation renews itself, when what is finished inevitably recedes, and the sacred forces of healing astonish us with the unending promise of love and life. When we gather together to worship and pray in this Sabbath time, we prepare our hearts and souls to be nourished and surprised by fruitful beginnings.

And so, only in the soil of Sabbath tranquillity can we seed the possibility of beginning a new day, a new week— even a new life—again and again, each time with fresh eyes, rested and refreshed, born within the completely gratuitous sanctuary of time.

Begin Again

It took a very long time for Jack to recover from the chemotherapy treatments for the tumor that threatened his brain. After the treatments were finally over, he would begin each morning with a Sabbath meal, a sacred, quiet time to begin the day fresh and new. He would squeeze fresh orange juice, and place it beside his meal on the breakfast table. Then he would wait, and while waiting, he would pray. He would reflect on the promise of the day, and wait—until the sun rose above a particular tree outside his window. Then the light from the sun would strike the orange juice, at which point, he said, it would "diffuse into orange, crystal light." Then he would drink from the glass, and begin the meal that began his day.

In the Buddhist community of Plum Village, Thich Nhat Hanh, a Vietnamese monk, periodically rings a Mindfulness Bell. Upon hearing the bell, everyone stops, and takes three silent, mindful breaths. Then they are free to continue their work, awakened ever so slightly by the Sabbath pause of mindfulness. We can choose anything to stop us like this—the telephone ringing, a stoplight when we are driving, whenever our hand touches a doorknob, before we eat or drink. Choose one common act during your day to serve as a Sabbath pause. Whenever this arises—whenever you touch a doorknob or hear the telephone—simply stop, take three silent, mindful breaths, and then go through the door or answer the phone. See how it changes you to take these tiny Sabbath moments every day.

IT IS GOOD

And God saw everything that he had made,
and behold, it was very good.

— GENESIS 1:31

O ur willingness to rest depends on what we believe
we will find there. At rest, we come face-to-face with
the essence of life. If we believe life is fundamentally
good, we will seek out rest as a taste of that goodness.
If we believe life is fundamentally bad or flawed, we
will be reluctant to quiet ourselves, afraid of meeting
the darkness that resides in things—or in ourselves.

In Genesis, a fundamental goodness is presumed
throughout the creation story. At every juncture God
acts, steps back, and rests. God invokes the light, separates it from the darkness—creating a conversational

rhythm between light and dark—and steps back. *And God saw that it was good*. Then God makes a place for heaven and earth, separates the sea from dry land—creating a tidal rhythm—and steps back. *And God saw that it was good*.

Then God made the sun and moon, creating a seasonal rhythmicity. And, stepping back, *God saw that it was good*. And so the story continues, emptiness giving birth to form, with the creation of living creatures, the beautiful birds that claim the air as their home, the many-colored fish and great whales, the cattle and insects, all the animals wild and free upon the earth. Then God creates man and woman in the likeness of God. *And God saw everything that he had made, and behold, it was very good*.

Sabbath rest invites us to step back, *and see that it is good*. Jews believe that on the Sabbath we are given an extra soul—the *Neshemah Yeterah*, or Sabbath soul—which enables us to more fully appreciate and enjoy the blessings of our life and the fruits of our labors. With this extra soul, like God on the Sabbath we, too, are more able to pause, and see how it is good.

Since I was a child I have felt this fundamental goodness in the world—in people, in life, in the earth. It is not something I learned, apprehended, or discovered. It was something I knew, like gravity, or wind. I have felt the truth of this goodness even when no external evidence suggested its presence. This is what drew me to the field of psychotherapy, and later to the ministry and spiritual practice. In psychotherapy training I gravitated toward those forms of healing that presumed this essential strength and wisdom in people, those methods that sought to affirm what was already whole and strong. I steadfastly believed, even as I worked in the midst of the most horrific sorrow—sexual abuse, alcoholism, poverty, illness—that there remained a persistent luminosity of spirit, an unquenchable resilience.

When I was young I had no way to speak of this goodness. Later, as a therapist, I was taught no official diagnostic name for this place. Only poetry and music, art and dance seemed to know of this vast and luminous country. Only in spiritual texts would I find such phrases as Thomas Merton's "hidden wholeness" or Tibetan Buddhism's "persistent luminosity." Through my seminary training and meditation practice I would learn that the spiritual traditions of the world dearly love this inner resilience, and call it by many names: inner light, still, small voice, Buddha Nature, Kingdom of God, Holy Spirit.

If we look deeply and carefully within all that is hurtful, ignorant, and wounded, we will eventually see the light of the world shine through. When Jesus says "You are the light of the world" he is reaffirming this persistent luminosity, our hidden wholeness. As children of a good and whole creation, we remain whole and good in spite of all our sorrows, sins, and weaknesses.

The Sabbath makes this very same presupposition. Sabbath time assumes that if we step back and rest, we will see the wholeness in it all. We will naturally apprehend the good in how things are, taste the underlying strength, beauty, and wisdom that lives even in the difficult days, take delight in the gift and blessing of being alive.

If we believe our soul is naturally luminous and that we are filled with innate, natural perfection, if we are the light of the world, then when we sink into quiet we return to peace. Conversely, if we believe creation is badly flawed, then we must avoid intimate contact with it. We greet silence with fear, afraid it will show us the broken center at the core of the world and of ourselves. Afraid of what we will find there, we avoid the stillness at all costs, keeping ourselves busy not so much to accomplish but to avoid the terrors and dangers of emptiness.

Jesus began his Sermon on the Mount—arguably the most important teaching of his life—by saying *Blessed are*. Blessed are the poor. Blessed are those who mourn. Blessed are the meek. He did *not* say "Blessed will be the poor when they finally achieve a certain level of economic independence." He did not say "Blessed will be those who mourn after they have endured their period of unspeakable grief and received support from their clergy or family." He did not say "Blessed will be the meek after they graduate from assertiveness training, and claim their inner strength."

He said blessed *are*. Not "they will one day be blessed," but they are blessed *right now*. The poor are blessed, even in their poverty. Those who mourn are blessed, even in their grief. The meek, the merciful, even those who are persecuted—blessed, blessed, blessed. Not later. Not when their trials are over. Not when they are fixed. Right here, right now. There is a blessing for you here, now, in this very moment.

All Jesus' teaching seems to hinge on this singular truth concerning the nature of life: It is all right. *Do not worry about tomorrow. I have come that you might have life abundantly. Be not afraid.* Over and over, in parable, story, and example, he insists that regardless how it goes for us, we are cared for, we are safe, we are all right. There is a light of the world, a kingdom of heaven inside us that will bear us up, regardless of our sorrow, fear, or loss. Do not wait to enjoy the harvest of your life; you are already blessed. *The kingdom of God is already here. It is within you and among you.*

Like the creator who steps back and sees that it is good, Jesus just as confidently insists we are already whole. Once we become aware of this teaching in the gospels, we find it everywhere. *Whoever has eyes, let them see, and ears, let them hear.* Do not wait to be joyful; take your portion now, take your rest and savor the delicious fruits of the kingdom. *Do you not say "There are yet four months, then comes the harvest"? I tell you, lift up your eyes, and see how the fields are already white for harvest. You are the light of the world. Rejoice always. Be of good cheer. Elijah has already come. You are already blessed.*

What if, as Thomas Merton insists, we harbor a hidden wholeness? What if, as the Buddhists insist, we are saturated with an innate natural perfection? What if, as Jesus insists, we are the light of the world? What if, as God insists, it is already good, very good?

In this light the Sabbath prescription is a loving reminder to take full advantage of a condition that already exists. At rest, our souls are restored. This is the only commandment that begins with the word "remember," as if it refers to something we already know, but have forgotten. It is good. It is whole. It is beautiful. In our hurry and worry and acquiring and working, we forget. Rest, take delight in the goodness of creation, and remember how good it is.

When people share with me their sorrow and suffering, at my best I am merely a faithful companion, watching for the wholeness embedded deep within their fear and confusion. For a time, all they can see or feel is the cold, cutting blade of their terror, the ache of despair, the burning sadness. My work is to be good company, to allow them to lean for a while on my unshakable belief in their inner fire. Even on the good days I cannot do more than this. Then, slowly, in their own time, their bodies open, they begin to feel and taste the possibility of this wholeness for themselves. This fundamental goodness always waits for us to discover it, if we will only gather together patiently, and listen.

On May 30, 1996, a fire ravaged Lama Mountain, home to many families in the hills of northern New Mexico, as well as to the Lama Foundation, a spiritual retreat center that had for years been a place of meditation and refuge for pilgrims from around the world. The fire was quick and furious. It destroyed dozens of homes and all but a few of the buildings at the retreat center. Three weeks after the fire, I walked the land with Owen Lopez, a close friend and director of the McCune Foundation in New Mexico. We were hoping, along with Bread for the Journey, to provide some emergency relief for the community, including quick restoration of water and electricity. Everywhere we looked we saw the color of charcoal, silver-gray-black, shiny, reflecting the light of the sun that filtered through charred and twisted branches. Just three weeks earlier, this was an inferno. But on this day there spread out before us a sea of green. Small oak seedlings, six to ten inches high, blanketed the forest floor. Without any human effort to clear or seed, already the earth was pushing out life. Creation creates life at every revolution; it is incapable of doing otherwise. Were we to reduce the planet to cinders, a holocaust of ignorance and greed, still the universe would create life from the ashes of our clumsiness.

Sabbath is a day we walk in the forest, walk among the fruits of our harvest and the ruins of our desperations, and see what lives. On the Sabbath, we rest. And see that it is good.

Blessing

My friend Ethan celebrates the Sabbath meal with his wife and daughter. It is traditional, before the meal begins, to put your hand on your children and give them a blessing. Ethan says this is his favorite moment of Sabbath. "The candles and the wine are sweet, but when I put my hand on my daughter's head and bless her, and offer a prayer for her strength and happiness, I can feel all the generations of parents who have blessed their children, everyone who has come before, and everyone who will come after."

Maria at Santo Domingo pueblo offers a blessing of cornmeal to the four directions before she begins the family meal.

Kalu Rinpoche, visiting an aquarium in Boston, kept stopping to put his fingers to the glass of each tank, quietly blessing every fish as he walked. *May you be happy. May you be at peace.*

Sharon Salzberg suggests we practice guerrilla compassion—silently blessing people on line at the bank, at the supermarket, in the cars next to us in traffic. Each blessing a tiny Sabbath, a secret sanctuary offered to a hurried and unsuspecting world.

There are many ways to offer your blessing. You may bless your children, your lover, your friend, by placing your hand on their head, and offering a prayer for their healing, their well-being, their happiness. Let them feel the truth of your prayer in their bodies. When this happens, many report feeling the physical

*blessing actually enter their body. It is as precious as it is free—
completely gratuitous.*

*Another practice invites us to bless strangers quietly, secretly.
Offer it to people you notice on the street, in the market, on the
bus. "May you be happy. May you be at peace." Feel the blessing move through your body as you offer it. Notice how you both
receive some benefit from the blessing. Gently, almost without
effort, each and every blessing becomes a Sabbath.*

FEAR OF REST

Rabbi Levi saw a man running in the street, and asked him, "Why do you run?" He replied, "I am running after my good fortune!" Rabbi Levi tells him, "Silly man, your good fortune has been trying to chase you, but you are running too fast."

— TRADITIONAL TALE

My friend Marilyn is a devoted massage therapist. She is very kind and works very hard. She serves in the poorest sections of San Francisco, offering her services for free to those most in need. In seedy residential hotels, where there are people dying of AIDS or suffering with tuberculosis, she goes from the room of one sick person to another, massaging, rubbing the salve of good care into their isolated dying bodies.

When Marilyn and I talk on the phone, she often sounds exhausted. I invite her to spend a day on the beach. She says she can't. She has too much work, too many people to meet, too many things to do. She is almost weeping, such is her need to rest, but she has no inner permission to stop working, even for an afternoon.

Marilyn cares for others with great conviction. But she does not care for herself with the same conviction. She feels her time at rest will somehow take away from those in need, those whom she truly loves and hopes to serve. She assures me she is all right, and in many ways I know that she is. But if she does not rest, how soon will she burn out, and who will care for those who need her then?

Shortly before Jesus was killed, he was sharing a meal with his followers at the home of Simon, a leper. A woman arrived, bearing an alabaster flask containing expensive ointment. She broke open the exquisite flask and anointed Jesus' head with the precious oil. His disciples were very angry with Jesus, saying: *Why this waste? This ointment might have been sold for a large sum, and given to the poor.* But Jesus responded, *Why do you trouble this woman? She has done a beautiful thing for me. You always have the poor with you, but you will not always have me.*

What is Jesus saying—not to worry about the poor? Of course not; his entire ministry is about service and kindness for those in need. He is saying that a life of compassion must include compassion for all beings, including the giver.

Our reluctance to rest—our belief that our joy and delight may somehow steal from the poor, or add to the sorrows of those who suffer—is a dangerous and corrosive myth, because it creates the illusion that service to others is a painful and dreary thing. Jesus says there will always be opportunities to be kind and generous. Just as there is a time for every purpose under heaven, so is there a time for nourishment and joy, especially among those who would serve.

Elaine, a well-respected therapist, came to me for counseling. As a woman from an abusive family, she had for many years struggled, grown, and overcome great sorrow. Now she was very strong. She was proud of what she had become. And while she had achieved professional success, she felt it was now time to explore her inner landscape, the more subtle movements of her spiritual life, and asked if I would be her spiritual director.

In spite of her significant career accomplishments, Elaine experienced a nagging emptiness. For some people, emptiness can feel fertile and spacious, alive with possibility, as a womb is ripe for the child to come. But others feel emptiness as an ache, a void; something painful, in need of being filled. When we are empty, we feel unhealed; when we are unhealed, we can feel unworthy. I sensed Elaine was uncomfortable and afraid of her emptiness.

"Tell me about your sense of worth," I said. She began by recounting her triumphs and successes, and her growing sense of personal and professional self-esteem. I stopped her. "I am not speaking about your self-esteem, which I am sure is justifiably strong, considering all you have done in your life. I am asking about the quiet times, the nights before sleep, the silent moments of the day when you are alone, when you are not a successful professional. In the Catholic Mass, there is a phrase spoken before one receives communion: *Lord, I am not worthy to receive you. But say the word, and I shall be healed.* For some reason, as we sit here together, I am reminded of that phrase. What do you think?"

Unexpectedly, she wept. Silent sobbing tears, for a long time. She looked at me surprised, as if I had both betrayed and loved her, hurt and thanksgiving rising together in her eyes. We had touched an emptiness that felt like a wound. It was deep inside her, and she did not know what it was. It frightened her.

This is one of our fears of quiet; if we stop and listen, we will hear this emptiness. If we worry we are not good or whole inside, we will be reluctant to stop and rest, afraid we will find a lurking emptiness, a terrible, aching void with nothing to fill it, as if it will corrode and destroy us like some horrible, insatiable monster. If we are terrified of what we will find in rest, we will refuse to look up from our work, refuse to stop moving. We quickly fill all the blanks on our calendar with tasks, accomplishments, errands, things to be done—anything to fill the time, the empty space.

But this emptiness has nothing at all to do with our value or our worth. All life has emptiness at its core; it is the quiet hollow reed through which the wind of God blows and makes the music that is our life. Without that emptiness, we are clogged and unable to give birth to music, love, or kindness. All creation springs from emptiness: *In the beginning, God created the heavens and the earth. The earth was without form, and void* . . .

Juanita is a Native American woman who leads people on vision quests—journeys into the wilderness, where they live for three days, alone, listening for the teachings that arise when one embarks on a sacred pilgrimage. What people are most afraid of, she tells me, is not so much the dangers that lurk in the wilderness, the wild animals, the darkness and cold. Most are far more anxious about having to confront whatever will come up in the empty space, when they are quiet and alone. Who knows what terror lurks in the anonymous solitude? What voices will arise in the silence? At the very same time, she says, people are afraid of what will not come up. What if I have no vision at all? What if there is nothing of value in my heart and soul, no strength, no voice of guidance, no wisdom at all—just an empty, hollow echo?

Emptiness is the pregnant void out of which all creation springs. But many of us fear emptiness. When we first glimpse emptiness, we taste the death in it. It feels like an abyss, a sheer drop into eternity, a dangerous negation of all that is alive, visible, safe, and good. We prefer to remain in the realm of form, surrounded by things we can see and touch, things we imagine are subject to our control.

I stumbled on emptiness one winter in Massachusetts. I was a visitor at a three-month silent meditation retreat at the Insight Meditation Society, a Buddhist retreat center in Barre. As a guest, I arrived after two hundred people had been sitting in silent meditation for nine weeks. When I first entered the meditation hall, I felt as though a warm wind was pressing on my chest, pushing me backward, forcing me to regain my balance. The silence of two hundred quietly breathing beings was viscerally palpable—silence that filled the air more surely than if it had been completely empty.

I took a place in the rear of the hall, and for a few days practiced in the company of these dedicated pilgrims. Vipassana meditation requires simply noting the rising and falling of the breath, and with it the arising and falling away of thoughts, sensations, feelings, returning to the breath again and again. One afternoon, completely unbidden, came emptiness. I felt a spaciousness beyond measure. For no reason I could fathom I felt how all things dissolve into nothingness, and arise again—people, buildings, the blanket covering my legs, thoughts, feelings, passion, ideas, my body, my loved ones, the earth itself, all simply forms that would, in their time, inevitably dissolve again into emptiness. The terror of the void was not there; I felt more liberated than frightened. In a way, everything was already over, all life destined to disassemble into emptiness. Suddenly, there was nothing left to worry about.

Kabbalists call this place the most intuitive and intimate relationship with God—the *ein sof*, literally, no limit, or infinite. It is that place that is both full of God and completely empty—because at that level there is no "thing" for God to be. There is only quiet, spaciousness, being. As the poet Paul Valéry said, "God made everything out of nothing, but the nothing shows through."

At a retreat, a doctor took me aside and confessed that for him, and for many of his friends and colleagues in medicine, part of their rush and hurry is fear of the terrible things they will feel in the quiet. They are so close to so much suffering and loss, they are afraid that if they stop, even for a moment, the sheer enormity of sorrow will suffocate and overwhelm them. The busyness of the medical model is in part a defense mechanism, a way to skate over the rampant, tender uncertainties of the practice of human healing.

Thus do our unspoken fears and sadnesses speed up our

lives. We are terrified of the painful grief that is hot to touch, sharp and piercing, so we keep moving, faster and faster, so we will not feel how sad we are, how much we have lost in this life: strength, youthful playfulness, so many friends and lovers, dreams that did not come true, all that have passed away. When we stop even for a moment, we can feel the burning, empty hole in our belly. So we keep moving, afraid the empty fire of loss will consume us.

When I was a boy I learned to skip stones across a lake. If I threw the stone fast and true, it could skip clear to the other side, barely getting wet. But if I threw it too slowly, it hit the water once and disappeared. We do not want to disappear. If we slow down we might be pulled by some gravity to the bottom of our feelings, we might drown in all we have lost. So we keep moving, never finding refuge, never touching the tendernesses that propel us into a life of speedy avoidance.

While our speed may keep us safe, it also keeps us malnourished. It prevents us from tasting those things that would truly make us safe. Prayer, touch, kindness, fragrance—all those things that live in rest, and not in speed. Only when we take refuge in rest can we feel the company of the angels that would minister to us, regardless of what we were given. In the stillness there are forces and voices and hands and nourishment that arise, that take our breath away, but we can never know this, *know* this, until we rest. This is what Jesus talks about when he speaks of the Kingdom of God. It is the Promised Land of the Hebrews, flowing with milk and honey. It is the Pure Land of the Buddha, what all the saints talk about, this place of safety and serenity, available and prepared for us, if we will only stop, and rest.

ANOTHER LOSS TO STOP FOR

Against such cold and mercurial mornings,
watch the wind whirl one leaf
across the landscape,
then, in a breath, let it go.
The color in the opaque sky
seems almost not to exist.

Put on a wool sweater.
Wander in the leaves,
underneath healthy elms.
Hold your child in your arms.

After the dishes are washed,
a kiss still warm at your neck,
put down your pen. Turn out the light.

I know how difficult it is,
always balancing and weighing,
it takes years and many transformations;
and always another loss to stop for,

to send you backwards.

Why do you worry so,
when none of us is spared?

—JILL BIALOSKY

Silence

When Eugene Peterson served as pastor of a church in Maryland, he took his Sabbath on Monday. He and his wife regularly packed lunches and binoculars into their backpacks, and drove a short way to a trailhead that meandered along a river or into the mountains. Before they began the hike, they would read a psalm, and then pray. After that, they hiked in complete silence for the next two or three hours, until they stopped for lunch. "We walk leisurely," he writes, "emptying ourselves, opening ourselves to what is there: fern shapes, flower fragrances, birdsong, granite outcropping, oaks, and sycamores, rain, snow, sleet, wind." When it was time for lunch, they broke the silence with a prayer of blessing for the food, the river, the forest. Then, free to talk, they shared their bird sightings, observations, feelings, and thoughts.

This kind of silence alters perception. We see differently in silence, when we are not expected to comment, analyze, or respond. The Buddhist precept of Right Speech includes the concept of refraining from speaking words that are not absolutely necessary. Things find their way deeper into our body when we are not in such a hurry to spit them back out.

Mother Teresa said, "God is the friend of silence." Things are born in quiet that cannot be heard in the din of our overly verbal days. Arsenius, one of the early Christian Desert Fathers, said, "I have often repented of having spoken, but never of having kept silent."

Sabbath time is enriched by some period of intentional silence. Choose a period of time or an activity—such as a walk or hike, alone or with someone you love—when you will refrain from speech. Notice what arises in silence, the impulse to speak, the need to judge or respond to what you see, hear, feel. Notice any discomfort that arises when you are not free to speak. When I first went to a monastery, the Great Silence between evening meal and breakfast seemed unbearable. Later, during a ten-day silent meditation retreat, I was convinced that the other retreatants—also silent—were all angry, or somehow mad at me. I could not rely on my wit, charm, or intellect to engage them. For the first few days I resented the silence. Now, after years of practice, I seek out silences, I delight in them. They seem sweet, safe, a Sabbath, a genuine sanctuary in time.

DORMANCY

If you want to become full,
let yourself be empty.
If you want to be reborn,
let yourself die.
— TAO TE CHING

Unlike humans, birds, or animals, perennial plants are fixed for life, and cannot migrate. Dormancy allows plants and their seeds to develop stress-resistant annual resting periods. When adverse conditions such as cold or drought arise, the plant ceases to receive its cues from the external environment and focuses inward, receiving its vital direction from ancient inner rhythms. Seeds may maintain dormancy even during favorable conditions, in order to give them time to fully mature.

Dormancy maximizes the seed's strength and hardiness, making it less susceptible to climactic extremes. In a given season this may diminish the yield, but it is a rhythm designed less for quick profit, and more for an abundance over eternity.

During the initial stage of dormancy—called *quiescence*—the plant slows in response to environmental cues. If there is too much cold or not enough light, a Douglas fir seedling will become quiescent, and cease its growth. But if those conditions change—a cold spring warms, a neighboring tree is cut down—new buds will elongate and a second flush of shoot growth will develop.

But the second stage of dormancy—called *rest*—is controlled not from without but from within. A seedling in the resting stage will not grow, no matter how favorable the environment. A warm January will not tempt it out; it heeds an inner clock, and emerges from dormancy only in the fullness of time, under the most deeply favorable conditions. This aids in the safe and healthy propagation of life.

In a similar fashion, when mammals hibernate in winter, their body temperatures drop to just above freezing, and their hearts beat very slowly. A woodchuck's body temperature may drop more than thirty degrees Celsius. The jumping mouse's tiny heart, which normally beats between five hundred and six hundred times per minute, slows to thirty beats per minute during hibernation. The animal survives on energy reserves stored in the body during summer and fall.

So when we see Jesus withdraw from the press of the crowds and retreat to a place of rest, he is not simply taking a well-deserved break from his useful but exhausting ministry. He is honoring a deep spiritual need for a time dedicated not to accomplishment and growth, but to quiescence and rest. His disciples cannot comprehend his leaving—there are still lepers to heal, blind that need to see, and the hungry to be fed. When Jesus slips away, they run about in search of him—doesn't he realize there is much good work to be done?

Soon enough, Jesus rests in death. Like a seed planted in fertile ground, he must die to bear fruit. *Unless a grain of wheat falls into the earth and dies, it remains alone; but if it dies, it bears much fruit.* And so Jesus dies, and lies dormant for three days. Without this dormancy, the resurrection of new life would be impossible.

If God raised Jesus in three days, surely he could have been raised in two, or one, or even been made invincible. So why sentence him to death for three days? Because everything, even the anointed of God, must rest, even in death.

Unless the grain falls into the earth and dies, there will be no harvest. These three days are the necessary dormancy of a Sabbath, an emptiness in which Jesus may be reborn, and take on a new form. All form is either arising or falling away. And between falling away and arising again, there is an inevitable dormancy, the *ein sof,* the emptiness of God.

The Sabbath Box

My friends Zalman and Eve faithfully keep the Sabbath. While I was visiting them last spring, they told me that in some families it is customary to make a Sabbath box to hold all the equipment you do not need on the Sabbath—pens, car keys, wallets, etc. "On Friday," they explained, "someone stands at the door with the Shabbos box and as people enter the house for the evening meal, they put in anything they know should not be taken into sacred space. Then, stripped of all our tools and machines, we can truly pray, *God, there is nothing I can do about these concerns, so I know it is in your hands.*"

Make a Sabbath box. When you set aside time for Sabbath— whether it is an hour, a morning, or a day—put in the box those things you do not want to use. For some, a computer or telephone will be too cumbersome, but something symbolic—an address book or a floppy disk—can serve as a physical reminder of what we leave behind when we enter sacred rest.

You can also use the Sabbath box to hold all the things you feel you have left undone. Perhaps write on a small piece of paper a word or phrase that signifies a particular worry or concern you would like to leave behind for the time being. Then light a candle, alone or with friends. Let each of you speak about those things that are left to do, and as the candle burns, allow the cares to melt away. Do not be anxious about tomorrow, said Jesus. The worries of today are sufficient for today. Whatever remains to be done, for now, let it be. It will not get done tonight. In Sabbath time we take our hand off the plow, and allow God and the earth to care for what is needed. Let it be. Then, at the end of your Sabbath time, be aware of how you open the box, and how you respond to what you receive back into your life.

RHYTHM

THE RHYTHM OF CREATION

To everything there is a season,
a time for every purpose
under heaven.

— ECCLESIASTES 3:1

Because a team of dedicated doctors and nurses skillfully treated my pneumonia—and through an intricate web of blessing and grace—I survived this most intimate conversation with my mortality. Still, for several months after I left the hospital, I continued to feel a weight of lingering weariness as my body worked to repair and renew what had been so terribly damaged and infected. I moved slowly, and not often. The smallest tasks exhausted me, and even reading felt like work. I had to take naps every day.

There was a rhythm to my days; a good day was

inevitably followed by a bad day; a time of clarity and strength invariably led to a time of weakness, and a recurring ache in my chest. I recovered in fits and starts, a gradual healing punctuated by periods of recurrence and remission.

But curiously, my most reliable feeling during this outwardly difficult period was an inward sense of peace. I felt a visceral surrender, deep in the cells of my body, a surrender into the arms of whatever or whoever was holding and healing me. It all seemed blessed, somehow, even the frustrating rhythms of strength and weakness. I regularly recalled the words of Dame Julian of Norwich, who asserted time and time again that regardless what sorrows or challenges may arise in our life, "All shall be well, and all manner of things shall be well."

Nevertheless, it became clear that I had to leave the high New Mexico desert, where the altitude and dry climate seemed to work against my healing. And so my family and I made plans to move to the ocean, where the lower altitude and soothing moisture would support the work of my body in regaining its strength. It was this sad necessity that demanded we leave behind many good and beloved friends, and make a pilgrimage to the edge of the great sea, to the coast of northern California.

Now, every day we walk along the ocean. Walking on Stinson Beach, not far from our little house, I cannot help but feel time move in cycles. Endlessly, wave after wave, the water climbs up the beach and recedes, threatens and calms, choppy and still, a relentless music of rhythmic change. Driftwood, flotsam, jetsam, shell, and stone are tossed up and then swallowed back down, things come and go, a furiously reliable dance of tidal impermanence.

Here, if there is such a thing as time, it surely cannot be linear. Einstein shattered our complacency when he showed us that light itself can bend, and time along with it. Can this truly be news? Everything begins and ends, and begins again, says the preacher in Ecclesiastes: "What has been is what will be, and what has been done is what will be done; and there is nothing new under the sun."

Perhaps the most recognizable quality of creation is this rhythmicity. The pulsing light and dark, expansion and contraction, the seasons and tides, the cycles of growth and dormancy, of life, death, and regeneration are unmistakable characteristics of all living things, from the smallest microbe to the largest galaxy.

The fruit contains the seed, and the seed contains the fruit. What we harvest in this season provides the seed for the next season. In Sabbath time we taste the fruit of our labor, and prepare the seeds for the week to come. If we are too busy, if we do not rest, we miss this rhythm. One day we look up and it is winter, and where are the fall days, brisk and clear, leaves ablaze? How did we spend them, what were we doing?

We do not gauge the value of the seasons by how quickly they progress from one to the next. Every season brings forth its bounty in its own time, and our life is richer when we can take time to savor the fruit of each. In the fall we chop and carry our wood, gather the harvest, rake leaves, prepare our home for winter, and give thanks. In winter we are dormant, a time for quiet generosities, and reflection on the endurance of inner light in the midst of darkness.

In spring we prepare the soil for planting, we prune what has been lost or dried up, we feed the soil and plant what is needed, and take delight in the flowers. In summer, we tend the garden, watch for weeds and crowding, thin what needs air and sun, at rest in the freedom of long days and warm nights, losing ourselves in the gift of sweet air and time.

So it is with the seasons of our children's lives, with each passing year a different kind of care, now more holding, now more letting go. Successes are replaced by tender insecurities, confidence turns to awkwardness, until new triumphs straighten the spine and fill the emerging soul with courage. Ever-changing qualities of attention are called forth, and love is offered in its season, now soft and yielding, now firm and resolute. All things require a particular kind of care, and move on. We offer our care and attention in this particular season, this particular moment, doing what is placed before us to do, with simple courage and no small faith.

When we know the seasons of things, we can feel their timing, their readiness. There is less pushing, more waiting to see what is necessary. When we feel these rhythms in our bodies, we are like a woman who knows a child is growing in her womb, but knows equally well that the time for her labor is yet far off. She is content to wait, knowing that every morsel of food she eats prepares the way for a child who will be born and go to school, perhaps marry, eventually grow old. All our work is fruitful in its season. We can taste the peach in the turning of the compost, smell the apple pie as we water the soil deep to the roots, feel the juice of the plum running down our chin as we spread manure.

At Bread for the Journey we have learned to feel the timing of people, of communities, as they become ripe and ready, each in their season, for healing. There is a deeper timing at work, a *kairos*, a fullness of time, when abused women have had enough and are ready to stand up and make a new life; when parents have seen enough children turn to drugs and so resolve to become mentors for those young girls and boys who need guidance and courage; when people, tired of being isolated, gather together to build a community center, a weaving cooperative, a day-care center. When they come to us, they are saturated with the fullness of all their dreams and disappointments, resurrections and resolutions. At last, in this very moment, the harvest is ready, and they want now, this day, to begin to build a better world.

We have learned to know this moment; if we are prepared to join them when they are ready, flush with courage and kindness, with a single act of generosity, the right gift at the right time, whole worlds can truly be saved.

When we live without listening to the timing of things— when we live and work in twenty-four-hour shifts without rest—we are on war time, mobilized for battle. Yes, we are strong and capable people, we can work without stopping, faster and faster, electric lights making artificial day so the whole machine can labor without ceasing. But remember: *No living thing lives like this.* There are greater rhythms that govern how life grows: circadian rhythms, seasons and hormonal cycles and sunsets and moonrises and great movements of seas and stars. We are part of the creation story, subject to all its laws and rhythms.

When we rest, we can relish the seasons of a moment, a day, a conversation. In relationships, we sense the rhythms of contact and withdrawal, of giving and receiving, of coming close, pulling away, and returning. To surrender to the rhythms of seasons and flowerings and dormancies is to savor the secret of life itself.

Many scientists believe we are "hard-wired" like this, to live in rhythmic awareness, to be in and then step out, to be engrossed and then detached, to work and then to rest. It follows then that the commandment to remember the Sabbath is not a burdensome requirement from some law-giving deity—"You ought, you'd better, you must"—but rather a remembrance of a law that is firmly embedded in the fabric of nature. It is a reminder of how things really are, the rhythmic dance to which we unavoidably belong.

The Sabbath Walk

The story is told of a South American tribe that went on a long march, day after day, when all of a sudden they would stop walking, sit down to rest for a while, and then make camp for a couple of days before going any farther. They explained that they needed the time of rest so that their souls could catch up with them.

The Sabbath walk is easily the most popular and beloved exercise among those who attend our retreats. It is a walk without any purpose, no need for insight or revelation. Simply let your soul catch up with you.

For thirty minutes walk slowly and silently—preferably outside in nature, but it can also be done indoors—without trying to get anywhere. It is more of an amble, a stroll. Let your senses guide your walk. If you are drawn to a leaf, a stone, a color, a chink in the concrete, a shape in the floor, the fragrance of the grass, simply stop, and linger, and allow the moment to be, to smell or touch or thoroughly observe whatever is available for you, to hear what it says, to see what it looks like, to feel what it has to say or teach. Do not hurry. There is no place to go. Take all the time you need to hear its secrets. Then when it is time, when the rhythm of being there gives way to the rhythm of moving along, when it is time to begin again, simply move on. Follow your own timing and curiosity. When you are called to stop, stop and investigate. When you are called to begin again, move on. That is all.

At the end of thirty minutes, notice what has happened to your body, your mind, your sense of time.

INNER MUSIC

Whoever has ears, let them hear.

— LUKE 8:8

Carolus Linnaeus, an eighteenth-century Swedish botanist, became so enamored with the rhythmicity in plants that he grew a garden that could tell time. He planted flowers that opened or closed their blossoms an hour apart, from morning to evening throughout the day.

All life vibrates to this inner music. The daily rhythms of many living things approximate a twenty-four-hour cycle, even when isolated in a laboratory. These circadian rhythms (from *circa*, "about," and *dies*, "daily") live deep in the body, are nearly impervious to alteration, and refuse to be extinguished. In normal daylight, mice in laboratories begin running on an exercise wheel about dusk, run intermittently through the night, and sleep during the day. Even when their cages are kept artificially dark for long periods, the mice maintain this circadian rhythm for several weeks.

Sometimes when I walk the beach at night, there is a luminescence in the waves, a microscopic alga that illuminates at night. This algae is nonluminescent during the day—even under artificially darkened laboratory conditions. Circadian rhythms will *entrain*, or adjust, to an artificial light-dark cycle—*but only if it does not deviate drastically from a twenty-four-hour cycle*. A test animal exposed to eleven hours of light and eleven hours of dark will gradually entrain to a twenty-two-hour cycle; if exposed to thirteen hours each of light and dark it will entrain to a twenty-six-hour cycle. But as soon as the artificial cycle is removed, the natural cycle returns. If the cycle is varied too much—if we try to entrain an organism to a thirty-, thirty-five-, or forty-hour cycle— the creature will soon give up trying to adjust, and return again to its original twenty-four-hour rhythm.

Photoperiodism describes an organism's ability to respond to varying periods of light and dark. Deciduous trees drop their leaves under the influence of the shorter days of autumn, and grow leaves again during the lengthening days of spring. Florists often use this photoperiodism to "trick" greenhouse plants into producing blossoms out of season by exposing them to unseasonable periods of artificial light.

Most organisms have more than one circadian rhythm. In human beings, different circadian rhythms govern the wake-sleep cycle, glandular secretions, highs and lows in body temperature, and the retention and excretion of urine. Despite all external manipulations of light, hours of sleep, or changes in nutrition, even under the most constant laboratory conditions, no organism can ever be completely entrained away from its true inner rhythm.

Just as we use this inner pulse for our survival, we also

use it to find our way in the world. Most animals navigate using natural rhythm and seasonal information such as tides, blooming vegetation, climatic conditions, sound, and light to orient themselves. Using circadian rhythms, animals gauge the angle of the sun above the horizon and combine it with the timing of light and darkness to get an accurate sense of their position.

Oysters open their shells when the moon is high. The chambered nautilus forms a new chamber in its spiraled shell every lunar month. Bees respond to the polarization of sunlight and orient themselves by the pattern it forms in a blue sky, even when the sun is behind the clouds.

There is a hum the earth makes. When seasonal winds pass over wave and mountain all across the earth and sea, a sound is born, a low-frequency pulsation audible to migrating birds thousands of miles away. By listening to the music of the earth, birds find their way home. Many birds also possess an inner orientation to true north; when they fly at night, they use the patterns and movements of the stars to guide their flight. Even in a planetarium, with the night sky projected on the ceiling, birds fly in rhythm with the seasonal stars.

We are blessed with these inner rhythms that tell us where we are, and where we are going. No matter, then, our fifty- and sixty-hour work weeks, the refusing to stop for lunch, the bypassing sleep and working deep into the darkness. If we stop, if we return to rest, our natural state reasserts itself. Our natural wisdom and balance come to our aid, and we can find our way to what is good, necessary, and true. We cannot be permanently entrained away from our natural rhythm.

But in the rush and pressure of modern life, we can refuse to listen.

The Cadence of Breath

Oscar Castro-Neves is an accomplished guitarist and composer. He writes musical scores for movies. He says it is common in a dramatic scene to gradually bring the music to crescendo, and then stop—rest—silence. "Whatever is spoken on the screen in that silence is heard more clearly, more powerfully; the words are lent an additional potency, because they are spoken out of the silence. When you listen to music," he counsels me, "listen to the cadence of rest." Then he gives me an example I can understand. "Martin Luther King, the most famous speech of his life. Listen to the cadence: *Free at last.* (Rest) *Free at last.* (Rest) *Thank God almighty, we are free at last.*"

At a retreat Seiji tells me he stayed up all night long, in the middle of the forest, waiting to hear the singular moment, early in the morning, when all the birds would begin to sing. He waited patiently in the silent stillness. Then, long before sunrise, "I heard the sound of a gentle inhale, as if all the trees around me, together, took a long, deep breath." All at once, he said, as if in unison with the exhale, the birds commenced their morning symphony.

One beautiful form of meditation is to simply follow the breath. Sit comfortably, and close your eyes. Let yourself become aware of the physical sensation of the breath, feeling the shape, texture, and duration of the inhale and the exhale. Do not change your breathing, do not strain or push in any way. Simply watch the breath breathe itself. Feel the rhythm of the breath, feel its timing, the end of the exhale, the readiness to inhale. When the mind wanders—as it will—do not worry. Simply return your awareness to the breath. Silently note each inhale or exhale, mentally noting in, out or rising, falling. Do this for five minutes at first. What do you notice about the rhythm of rest in your breathing? What do you notice about the rhythm of breath in your body?

HURTLING TOWARD THE
ESCHATON

That which has been is what will be,
that which is done is what will be done,
and there is nothing new under the sun.
— ECCLESIASTES 1:9

During the time of Jesus, Palestine was a place of wonder and anticipation, filled with miracle workers and prophesies of a Messianic Age. It was commonly believed in first-century Palestine that the end of history must be near, and that the Messiah would herald the coming of the *eschaton*, a Greek term meaning "the end time." Into this atmosphere came Jesus, a wise and gifted teacher. When his followers listened to his parables and stories, they could not help but hear them in terms of the prevailing messianic predictions. If Jesus was a messenger of the spirit, if he was a child

of the Creator, if he was divinely ordained and inspired—
then he must be the Messiah who would signal the coming of
the end time. Most of Jesus' followers could not help but
understand his words, actions, and teachings in that eschato-
logical context.

Because of this, the disciples' own teaching took on a
quality of desperate, imminent salvation. The scriptures and
epistles of early Christian apostles ring with exhortations to
repent, the end is near, and the time is soon coming when
Jesus will return in his Glory and judge the world. Many,
including the apostle Paul, were convinced they would still be
alive when Jesus returned.

Clearly this did not happen; neither did many other predictions by early church leaders of the imminence of the final
Kingdom of God as they understood it. They were not alone;
history is riddled with people, groups, and religions who have
predicted how history would end—usually in their favor,
often when they were alive, and universally accompanied by
the gleeful destruction of whomever they deemed their ene-
mies. But this is a very parochial view of time, to believe that
for as long as life has endured, time itself would choose to
come to its apocalyptic culmination simply because we have
now arrived.

However, the failure of the messianic prophecies does not
dissuade us from seeking the promised land, the perfect future, or the fountain of youth. In western civilization we
continue to be obsessed with eschatology. We still believe we
are the harbingers of a golden age; aided and abetted by the
breathtaking miracle of technology, we call our particular
messianic eschatology *progress*.

Progress is the road to the new and improved promised
land. At the end of progress, we will all have peak efficiency,
superior productivity, and an elevated standard of living. We
will have thoroughly mastered nature and all its inherent
problems, we will all live in a place and time in which all will
be well, all diseases cured, and all wars ended, with a chicken
in every pot. We are on the glory road, we are hurtling

toward the *eschaton*. There is no time to rest, because we are on a very important mission, to boldly go where no species has gone before. We never rest on our laurels, we never rest at all. Every moment is a necessary investment in the divinely ordained and completely unquestioned goal of progress.

What we are building for the future is infinitely more important than whatever we have right now. The eschatology of progress is an inflated pyramid scheme, where our riches exist always to be mined and harvested in the future, through endlessly expanding markets, not here, not now, but there, and later, we will see the promised land, we will make the big score, our ship will come in, we will get the pot of gold at the end of the rainbow, our time will come, we will strike it rich, we will hit the jackpot, we will be on easy street.

If the promised land is the good and perfect place, then where we are right now must be an imperfect place, a defective place. If the future is sacred, then the present is profane. Every day we are alive, every day we are not yet in paradise is a problem—our daily life is an obstacle in our way, it is another day short of the end time. Today—because it is not yet perfect—is always a bad day.

This means that we have to work hard and long and never, ever rest because our main task is to get the hell out of here. We cannot rest because we are in ungodly territory, the land of suffering and tribulation, and the sooner we get into the good and perfect future—the only place where we will ever be truly happy and at peace—the better off we will all be.

But there is no place to go. Every time we finally reach the future, it vanishes into the present. This perplexing tendency of the future to keep eluding us does not, of course, teach us to be more present, but rather to accelerate faster. We redouble our straining toward the future, never stopping to see where we are, never pausing to taste the fruits of our labor. Our true nourishment will come when we are successful, when we are rich, when we are saved, when it is our turn. Thus, satisfaction and delight are forever just out of reach.

So we despoil our nest, we ruin our air and soil, because it is all dispensable, we will not be here long, because here is no good, it is not where we are going, where we are going is good and holy and free and pure and perfect and it is not here and we are on our way and do not stop us do not get in our way or we will have to mow you down kill you ruin your country burn down your village to save it.

This, then, is the theology of progress. Only when we get to the end can we lie down in green pastures, be led beside still waters, and allow our soul to be restored. This is the psalm we sing when people have died. This is the psalm we save for death, because in the world of progress, you do not rest in green pastures, you do not lie beside still waters, there is no time. Never in this life, only in the next. Only when we get to the promised land.

But we must ask this question: What if we are not going anywhere? What if we are simply living and growing within an ever-deepening cycle of rhythms, perhaps getting wiser, perhaps learning to be kind, and hopefully passing whatever we have learned to our children? What if our life, rough-hewn from the stuff of creation, orbits around a God who never ceases to create new beginnings? What if our life is simply a time when we are blessed with both sadness and joy, health and disease, courage and fear—and all the while we work, pray, and love, knowing that the promised land we seek is already present in the very gift of life itself, the inestimable privilege of a human birth? What if this single human life is itself the jewel in the lotus, the treasure hidden in the field, the pearl of great price? What if all the way to heaven is heaven?

Sabbath challenges the theology of progress by reminding us that we are already and always on sacred ground. The gifts of grace and delight are present and abundant; the time to live and love and give thanks and rest and delight is now, this moment, this day. Feel what heaven is like; have a taste of eternity. Rest in the arms of the divine. We do not have miles to go before we sleep. The time to sleep, to rest, is now. We are already home.

Nature

Something will have gone out of us as a people if we ever let the remaining wilderness be destroyed; if we permit the last virgin forests to be turned into comic books and plastic cigarette cases; if we drive the few remaining members of the wild species into zoos or to extinction; if we pollute the last clear air and dirty the last clean streams and push our paved roads through the last of the silence. . . . And so that never again can we have the chance to see ourselves . . . part of the environment of trees and rocks and soil, brother to the other animals, part of the natural world and competent to belong in it.

We simply need that wild country available to us, even if we never do more than drive to its edge and look in. For it can be a means of reassuring ourselves of our sanity as creatures, a part of the geography of hope.

— WALLACE STEGNER

Almost every person who spoke to me about Sabbath said some time in nature is essential—it is singularly the most nourishing, healing Sabbath practice. One clergyman tells me, "When I spend any time at all in nature I open up, I rekindle a relationship with the natural world. I lose any sense of neediness, and the world opens herself to me. After a while, I feel there is nothing I am seeking, nothing I need." Leslie tells me that she and her husband always do something in nature—hike, go to the beach, anything that gets them outdoors. "We feel our bodies, the sensuality, we feel more grounded."

The Sabbath was born with the creation of the earth, so Sabbath time beats in intimate synchronicity with the rhythms of nature. Set aside a period of time, alone or with someone close to you, and walk, bike, sail, nap—anything that allows your body to be soothed by the enfolding nourishment of the earth. Spend as much time as possible in silence.

LET IT BE

Be content with what you have;
   rejoice in the way things are.
When you realize there is nothing lacking,
   the whole world belongs to you.
                    — LAO-TZU

There is astounding wisdom in the traditional Jewish Sabbath, that it begins precisely at sundown, whether that comes at a wintry 4:30 or late on a summer evening. Sabbath is not dependent upon our readiness to stop. We do not stop when we are finished. We do not stop when we complete our phone calls, finish our project, get through this stack of messages, or get out this report that is due tomorrow. We stop because it is time to stop.

Sabbath requires surrender. If we only stop when we are finished with all our work, we will never

82

stop—because our work is never completely done. With every accomplishment there arises a new responsibility. Every swept floor invites another sweeping, every child bathed invites another bathing. When all life moves in such cycles, what is ever finished? The sun goes round, the moon goes round, the tides and seasons go round, people are born and die, and when are we finished? If we refuse rest until we are finished, we will never rest until we die. Sabbath dissolves the artificial urgency of our days, because *it liberates us from the need to be finished*.

The old, wise Sabbath says: *Stop now*. As the sun touches the horizon, take the hand off the plow, put down the phone, let the pen rest on the paper, turn off the computer, leave the mop in the bucket and the car in the drive. There is no room for negotiation, no time to be seduced by the urgency of our responsibilities. We stop because there are forces larger than we that take care of the universe, and while our efforts are important, necessary, and useful, they are not (nor are we) indispensable. The galaxy will somehow manage without us for this hour, this day, and so we are invited—nay, commanded—to relax, and enjoy our relative unimportance, our humble place at the table in a very large world. The deep wisdom embedded in creation will take care of things for a while.

When we breathe, we do not stop inhaling because we have taken in all the oxygen we will ever need, but because *we have all the oxygen we need for this breath*. Then we exhale, release carbon dioxide, and make room for more oxygen. Sabbath, like the breath, allows us to imagine we have done enough work *for this day*. Do not be anxious about tomorrow, Jesus said again and again. Let the work of this day be sufficient.

When our will is bent toward a goal, we enter so deeply into our work that we soon feel this project or task is the only thing that truly matters. And in that moment—if we do our work well—we must focus in that way on the task before us. Yet the instant we put down the pen, close up the toolbox, or turn off the machines, we lift up our eyes and see the horizon, the place where sun and earth seem to touch—*I will lift up mine eyes unto the hills, from whence cometh my help*—and in that moment, we surrender. We feel how large the universe is, and how small our labors. Our work is simply one offering among countless others that have come before and will come again, when all we have planted has been grown, harvested, eaten, and forgotten.

When we stop, we see that the world continues without us; sweet humility and gentle mindfulness bequeath the grace to stop, and see that it is good, there is no need to keep pushing. When we stop, with no chores or agenda, we let our eyes rest, our bodies heal, our activities languish, and taste the fruits of our labor, as the Psalmist invites us: Be still, and know.

Henri Nouwen was a dear friend of mine, a brother, priest, and mentor. He was also a fiercely astute observer of our worried, overfilled lives. Henri insisted that the noise of our lives made us deaf, unable to hear when we are called, or from which direction. Henri said our lives have become absurd—because in the word *absurd* we find the Latin word *surdus*, which means *deaf*. In our spiritual life we need to listen to the God who constantly speaks but whom we seldom hear in our hurried deafness.

On the other hand, Henri was fond of reminding me that the word *obedient* comes from the Latin word *audire*, which means "to listen." Henri believed that a spiritual life was a pilgrimage from absurdity to obedience—from deafness to listening. If we surrender fully into Sabbath time, we can slowly move from a life so filled with noisy worries that we are deaf to the gifts and blessings of our life, to a life in which we can listen to God, Jesus, all the Buddhas and saints and sages and messengers who seek to guide and teach us.

The world seduces us with an artificial urgency that requires us to respond without listening to what is most deeply true. In Sabbath time, we cultivate a sense of eternity where we truly rest, and feel how all things can wait, and turn them gently in the hand until we feel their shape, and know the truth of them.

The theology of progress forces us to act before we are ready. We speak before we know what to say. We respond before we feel the truth of what we know. In the process, we inadvertently create suffering, heaping imprecision upon inaccuracy, until we are all buried under a mountain of misperception. But Sabbath says, Be still. Stop. There is no rush to get to the end, because we are never finished. Take time to rest, and eat, and drink, and be refreshed. And in the gentle rhythm of that refreshment, listen to the sound the heart makes as it speaks the quiet truth of what is needed.

Ette Hillesum was a thoughtful young Dutch woman, a victim of the Nazi concentration camps. In the diary she kept in the midst of the Nazi occupation, she describes the tender balance between her daily forebodings and her deeper search for peace:

> We have to fight them daily, like fleas, those many small worries about the morrow, for they sap our energies. . . . The things that have to be done must be done, and for the rest we must not allow ourselves to become infested with thousands of petty fears and worries, so many motions of no confidence in God. Ultimately, we have just one moral duty: to reclaim large areas of peace in ourselves, more and more peace, and reflect it towards others. And the more peace there is in us, the more peace there will also be in our troubled world.

Prayer

All over my native Austria the chorus of Angelus bells rises from every church steeple, at dawn, at high noon, and again before dark in the evening. At school one day—I was a first-grader then—I happened to stand by an open window on the top floor looking down on "the campus," you might call it, for ours was a big, beautiful school built by the Christian Brothers. It was noon. Classes had just finished and everywhere children and teachers came streaming out onto the courts and walkways. From so high up, the sight reminded me of an anthill on a hot summer day. Just then, the Angelus bell rang out from the church and at once all those busy feet down there stood still. "The angel of the Lord brought the message to Mary . . ." We had been taught to recite this prayer in silence. Then, the ringing slowed down; one last stroke of a bell and the anthill was swarming again.

Now, so many years later, I still keep that moment of silence at noon. Bells or no bells, I pray the Angelus. I let the silence drop like a pebble right into the middle of my day and send its ripples out over its surface in ever-widening circles. That is the Angelus for me; the Now of eternity rippling through time.

—BROTHER DAVID STEINDL-RAST

Prayer is like a portable Sabbath, when we close our eyes for just a moment and let the mind rest in the heart. Like the Muslims who stop to pray five times a day, like the Angelus, we can be stopped by a bell, a sunset, a meal, and we can pray. Something close to the heart, and simple. Perhaps a line from the Twenty-third Psalm, the Lord's Prayer, a short blessing: May all beings be happy, may all beings be at peace. Thank you, God, for this most amazing day. The Lord is my shepherd. Thy will be done.

Traditional Sabbaths are filled with prayers. But we can begin slowly, with a simple prayer, like a pebble dropped into the middle of our day, rippling out over the surface of our life.

THE BOOK OF HOURS

Sixty-six times have these eyes beheld the
    changing scenes of Autumn.
I have said enough about moonlight,
    Ask me no more.
Only listen to the voices of pines and cedars,
    when no wind stirs.

    — RYO-NEN (HER LAST COMPOSITION)

Fifteen years ago Henri Nouwen gave me a copy of
the Liturgy of the Hours, a collection of prayers that
mark each passing hour, day, week, month, and year.
Different prayers for different seasons, prayers to begin the day and prayers to settle us for sleep; prayers
for times of unspeakable sadness and mourning, and
prayers for times of great thanksgiving. Every hour is
punctuated with the deep rhythmicity of prayer.

I remember one morning driving back from the
beach, where Henri and I had spent the previous night
at a small cottage belonging to a member of our

church. We were driving on the highway just after dawn, dodging morning traffic, Henri beside me in the passenger seat, leading us both in morning prayer, reading from the Book of Hours. Henri rarely allowed an hour to pass without finding some opportunity for prayer.

I still have that same Book of Hours on my desk, and when it catches my eye I often find myself turning to the prayer for that morning, noon, midafternoon, or evening. There are prayers for feast days and holy days and Lent and Easter and Advent and all the markings on the circle of time. When I stop to pray, I feel my body release, disengage slightly from the rush of activity and progress, and float on the tides of a deeper time, tides that have borne up the lives of all who have prayed throughout eternity.

Every day, every year circles around the silent turning of cycles and rhythms. At Christmas we are reminded to look carefully, to remember that God can take birth where and when we least expect it, and to rejoice when we discover even the tiniest, infant manifestation of the divine. Hanukkah reminds us again and again that in the dark the light is born, that it is never fully extinguished, no matter how hopeless and impenetrable the darkness. The Crucifixion reminds us that all things must die, and Easter that all things will be reborn. Rosh Hashanah and Yom Kippur remind us that we must account for our lives, our actions, be mindful of what we have done, atone for our mistakes, and begin always and again anew. In the month of Ramadan we fast, and pray, and devote ourselves to a God who will not leave us comfortless. On Sabbath we rest, and remember that we are cared for.

Liturgical ritual is meant to be repeated. We are not supposed to do it right the first time, and then be done with it. We are not supposed to do it better each year until we get it perfect. This year's Easter does not have to be new and improved, more dramatic and moving than last year's. The perfection is in the repetition, the sheer ordinariness, the intimate familiarity of a place known because we have visited it again and again, in so many different moments.

Over the course of a lifetime there will be the sad Easter
and the joyous Easter, the thoughtful Easter and the hopeful
Easter, the transformative Easter and even the boring Easter.
This is not about progress, it is about circles, cycles, and
seasons, and the way time moves, and things we must remember, because with ever-faster turnings of the wheel it can
become easier to forget.

Ritual calls us back to the center, back to the breath, a
short meditation, a chant, a mantra. With each candle, song,
and prayer we are loosed from the anchor of habitual concern, and rest in the rhythm of eternity, enormous sweeps of
time that bear us up, in the divine inhale and exhale. We lean,
as in the traditional gospel hymn, "safe and secure from all
alarms; leaning, leaning, leaning on the everlasting arms."

When liturgy is ensnared by progress, all these quiet,
mystical qualities are replaced by responsibility and obligation. I have been part of so many little churches paralyzed by
the assumption that we must make this year's Christmas pag-
eant better, more dramatic, more impressive, more spectacu-
lar than the last. I have seen parents, children, and youth
ministers frantic, desperate, frustrated, and overwhelmed as
they try to make the "perfect" representation of an event that
was, at its origins, quiet, unassuming, unpredictable, sloppy,
and invisible. The same is true for Palm Sunday, even more
for Easter, piling on mountains of cute children's flowers,
butterflies, lilies, more of everything.

We must be willing to fall into life's rhythm, even if only
to pause for a word of thanks before a meal. The liturgical
year grants us this pearl of great price: *You are not going
anywhere. Millions have done this before you, and millions will
do it after you are gone. When you drink this cup, light this
candle, recite this prayer, there is sacredness and magic in it. It is
a gift for you, to help you remember who you are, and to whom
you belong. Come, and take your rest.*

OPENING WITHOUT WORDS

It is the beginning of May
and over near the statue of Moses,
raising his staff to something
none of us can see, hundreds of tulips
have broken through the dark earth
becoming every color they held inside
and quietly they ignore each other
in this chorus of oneness, bobbing gently,
as children race up to their splashes
of yellow and red, expecting the colors
to sing, and maybe they do in a song
only children can hear, and old men
amble through the rows, hands behind
their backs, as if in some European church
about to crumble, and this old white-haired
woman, with sheer wonder on her face,
sneaks up on the pink ones, her silent mouth
a flower, and, for the moment, we are all
opening without words, and her dog,
a pink-nosed spaniel, drops its ball
and rolls on its back slowly, and
my lover jumps out of her shoes,
pulls me by my sun-warmed hand
into the middle of a yellow patch,
and buries her face in them
and then she rises, a color
breaking ground herself,
pollen on her nose. Quietly,
we are saved, again.

—MARK NEPO

PRACTICE:

Lectio Divina

Cornelia is ninety-four years old. She is a beloved founding member of the board of Bread for the Journey. Every afternoon she rests—if she can, so busy is her daily schedule of appointments—because when she rests things fall away, she says, and come clearer. One of her favorite rituals is to read aloud. The last time I visited her she was reading the *Odyssey* aloud to herself, listening to the poetry of it, letting it carry her. Her voice is not exercised when she is alone, and the use of her voice is a soothing practice. And the ritual of reading aloud some beautiful or sacred passage changes the atmosphere, she says. It feeds the soul.

Lectio divina, or contemplative reading, is an ancient practice common to most religions. It begins with reading a short passage of scripture or other inspirational writing, and then quietly reflecting upon it—not analyzing or trying to figure out the meaning—but rather allowing it to quietly work on you, as leaven in the bread, as water on a stone. The key is to read slowly, chew over the words, and allow them to quietly nourish and heal you.

Choose a short piece of scripture for reflection. During Sabbath time I often choose the Twenty-third Psalm. I read it a few times silently, and then choose a phrase that speaks to me—"The Lord is my shepherd" is one that Henri Nouwen used as his mantra for two years. Others might be "I will dwell in the House of the Lord forever" or "My cup runneth over." Then, sit quietly or take a Sabbath walk, and allow the scripture to accompany you. Without grasping for meaning or answers, let the phrase live in the breath, using it to bring awareness back to this moment whenever the mind wanders. What do you notice about the words? How do they change? How do your feelings about each nuance shift over time?

One woman, who had cancer and was still undergoing many treatments, told me the word that spoke to her was simply the word surely. *As in, "Surely, goodness and mercy will follow me all the days of my life . . . ." Simply repeating the word* surely *brought her great comfort and peace.*

TIME

A LIFE WELL LIVED

If a country is governed wisely . . .
People enjoy their food,
take pleasure in being with their families,
spend weekends working in their gardens,
delight in the doings of the neighborhood.

        — TAO TE CHING

There is a grand and lively debate flourishing throughout the land, lamenting the tragic decline in our morality and values. Where in our political life— everyone cries in anguish—have our traditionally held values of honesty, courage, and integrity gone? Where in our civic life are the fundamental qualities of respect, deliberation, and wisdom? Where, in our personal lives, are the codes of individual responsibility and accountability, civility and compassion?

It is refreshing—and invigorating—to participate in a resurgence of conversation about the human qualities essential for a good and worthy civilization. But the pundits who frame these questions on radio and television, in books and magazines, rarely question the values of civilization itself, only the values of the people within it. At the least, this is misleading; at worst, it is dishonest, for it does not allow us to see the larger canvas on which this distressing evolution is painted.

All these "lost" values are human qualities that require time. Honesty, courage, kindness, civility, wisdom, compassion—these can only be nourished in the soil of time and attention, and need experience and practice to come to harvest. These are not commodities that can be bought, sold, or invested. They cannot be manufactured, advertised, or marketed. Our core human values, the deepest and best of who we are, require the nourishment of time and care, if we are to grow and flourish.

But we have traded our time for money. In fact, the catechism is quite specific: "Time is money." Our entire civilization is confirmed in this fundamental "value." When presented with a choice between time and money, it is best to trade up, to trade lesser-valued time for greater-valued money. It is seen as the prudent, superior, and necessary act.

In this atmosphere, what happens to the time, care, and attention absolutely required for cultivating our essential human values? They are traded away, desperately, enthusiastically, in the cathedral of the free and unrestricted marketplace. It is the temple to which we are all drawn to worship, bringing our offerings of time, and taking away the blessings of money.

The point is not that money is bad. Money allows us to participate in the national marketplace and to purchase all the basic goods and services we cannot provide for ourselves. But how much time should we trade for it? How do we decide when we have too much time and not enough money, and when do we know we have too much money and not enough time? In our culture we so overvalue money that this question is rarely asked.

People who have a lot of money and no time, we call "rich." And people who have a great deal of time but no money, we call "poor." A "successful" life is one in which one is always terribly busy, working hard, accomplishing great things, and making a great deal of money. The profoundly rich are put on the covers of magazines, their million- and billion-dollar fortunes, mansions, corporate acquisitions, and opulent life-styles are held up to the public eye as the model, the dream, the jackpot of a winning life. Best-selling books and television programs promise to reveal the secret formula for getting rich, making more money than you ever imagined, becoming a real success.

In the 1950's the national dialogue was preoccupied with very different concerns. Articles in magazines agonized over the perplexing dilemma looming ahead: What were we going to do with all our leisure time? Experts confidently predicted that—thanks to the efficiency of automation and the proliferation of near-miraculous labor-saving devices—we would all be working thirty-hour weeks, perhaps even twenty-hour weeks, and that we would be overwhelmed by the sheer weight of so much leisure time.

What happened? Essentially, we traded away all that nascent leisure time in exchange for more work and greater pay, so that we could afford to buy more and more products. In 1947, the average American adult spent $6,500 on material possessions, goods, and services. Today, adjusted for inflation, we spend an average of over $14,000 per adult. We spend twice as much for a larger house, and fill it with twice as many appliances, cars, clothes, and televisions.

When we are not using our time to get money, we are using time to spend money. Compared to Europeans, Americans spend three to four times as many hours per year shopping. Shopping has become a primary use of leisure time. With our few remaining free hours we scurry about in monstrous malls—our new civic centers—where we spend our money on goods and services we secretly hope will bring us peace, nourishment, or relief.

Look how we spend our summer vacations—if we are lucky enough to have a job that allows us to take time off in the summer. Gone are the lazy, languid weeks of summer, the hot days and long, warm nights, sitting on the porch, walking in the park, maybe putting together a pickup game of base-ball, or a simple picnic. Instead we buy ourselves a new and improved totally great summer—with boats, Jet Skis, Roller-blades, mountain bikes, rafting trips, six flags over Disney-land, all timed to never stop, not even for an instant. It seems almost pathetic, now, to suggest that we could ever have had a good summer by doing pretty much nothing at all.

Instead of taking the benefits of our modern technological civilization in the form of time, we converted the benefits into cash. This imbalance creates a time famine with innumerable consequences for our personal, family, and community life. For example, a 1995 study showed that adolescents who regu-larly spent time interacting with their families were more likely to become light users of alcohol, or not to drink at all. The less time parents had to "hang out" with their children, the more likely there would be an alcohol problem with the teenager in the family.

When we are tired from overwork, when we work fifty or sixty hours a week, how can we participate in family and civic life? Good citizenship requires time to listen to the fears and dreams of our neighbors, to care for our poor and hungry, to build and run good, wholesome schools and hospitals. Mark the steady decline in party membership, voter tallies, atten-dance at public meetings and school boards. It is not that we do not care. Indeed, we might be willing to send a check to this or that cause that we want to support. But where will the people come from who will run those groups? In the end, we cannot pay others to run a democracy for us.

Lorraine, an independent businesswoman, speaks elo-quently of the cost of a "successful" life: "You have to give up something to be a success in business. There's not time for everything. Me, I have very little time for my spiritual life. I don't have a civic life. And I do very little with friendships—

anything that doesn't have to do with business. I don't have time to cultivate relationships that aren't profitable."

The problem is not simply that we work too much, the problem is that we are working for the wrong reward. We are paid in the wrong currency. We reward the fruits of our labor and the sweat of our brow with money, goods, and services. We need to seek instead a more fertile, healing balance of payments—some of our pay in money, and some of our pay in time.

What if we were to expand our definition of wealth to include those things that grow only in time—time to walk in the park, time to take a nap, time to play with children, to read a good book, to dance, to put our hands in the garden, to cook playful meals with friends, to paint, to sing, to meditate, to keep a journal. What if we were to live, for even a few hours, without spending money, cultivating time instead as our most precious resource?

Although we purchase twice what we did in the 1950's, can we honestly say we are happier for it? Do we sense that our neighbors, friends, and family are more at peace, joyful, at ease? Do we feel in them a palpable sense of well-being and delight? If not, why not? Our cars are faster, our telephones reach farther, our computers are everywhere, our dishwashers are more efficient, our armies better equipped, our police have more weaponry, our medicines are more powerful, our interstate highways are bigger and reach farther, our buildings are safer, more modern, and temperature-controlled. We have, in short, everything we ever wanted. Or do we?

The Sabbath is a revolutionary invitation to consider that the fruits of our labor may be found in the restful and unhurried harvest of time. In time, we can taste the sweetness of peace, serenity, well-being, and delight. The truth must be told: With all the money in the world, and no time, we have nothing at all.

Play

Ed and Jill, years ago, decided they would not do any business on weekends, but devote their time to the children. When I ask Ed to play golf with me on a Sunday, he refuses, no regret, his family time is sacred. On weekends, I can go to their house any time and know they will be there. I stopped by on a Sunday last February when I was back in Santa Fe, and they fed me, and gave me tea, and I sat with their son Sam in his room and he showed me his school film projects. I could thoroughly enjoy those hours in the sanctuary of their welcoming home, knowing there would be no interruptions, nothing else would be more important than this.

I was discussing the dilemma of overwork with my friend George, who is president of a large university. In the many years I have known him, I have always found George to be essentially balanced and equanimous, even under the weight of great responsibility. I asked him how he managed to balance his tremendous workload with time for family. "I work long hours—but I also stop," he said. "I have never let work crowd out family time. And I am convinced almost nothing is worth losing sleep over."

At our house, the evenings are family time. We play cards, games, checkers, catch. After dinner and before bed no phones are answered, no business done.

When do you set aside time for play? How inviolable is it? Make sure to create a regular period for enjoying your children, spouse, or friends. Play nourishes our delight. When we engage in "purposeless" enjoyment of one another, we harvest some of the sweetest fruits of life.

SEIZE THE DAY

This is the day the Lord hath made;
let us rejoice and be glad in it.

—PSALM 118

On December 1, 1930, at the start of the Great Depression, W. K. Kellogg replaced the traditional three daily eight-hour shifts in his Battle Creek, Michigan, cereal plant with four six-hour shifts. By adding one entire shift, he reasoned, thirty percent more jobs would be added at the plant—jobs desperately needed by the unemployed in the city.

As Benjamin Hunnicutt describes in *Work Without End*:

Kellogg's six-hour day was an instant success, attracting national media coverage and the attention of Herbert Hoover's administration. Observers throughout the world speculated that Kellogg's experiment offered a practical way out of the depression and, in light of the fact that hours of labor had been steadily declining for over a century, was almost certainly a foretaste of things to come.

In a gesture of respect and civic decency, Kellogg also paid his workers for seven hours during the first year of the six-hour day, and in the second year wages were raised back to the level of the eight-hour day. This proved no economic loss to Kellogg. Through the introduction of new technology—and because of the new hours and work incentives—productivity increased dramatically. In essence, Kellogg shared the benefits of that increased productivity with his workers in the form of free time.

In 1932, the U.S. Department of Labor sent a research team to Battle Creek to interview Kellogg's workers. They found that nearly eighty-five percent preferred the six-hour shift, primarily because it provided "more time for family activities and home duties and leisure" and because it helped some of the unemployed find work. The great majority of the Kellogg workers used *freedom* or closely related words when the agents asked them to compare the eight-hour and six-hour shifts.

Talking to Hunnicutt a half-century later, workers recalled the pleasures of the six-hour shift:

> For Susan Smith, the extra time she had as a result of the six-hour shift allowed her to get her housework out of the way and get on to what she saw as the real part of the day: reading, walking, writing. She was self-educated, and it was in the few hours between routine housework and the job that she could keep the life of her mind and spirit alive, and find time to be involved in her community.
>
> Josephine Isley spoke enthusiastically about canning at

home during her early days at Kellogg's, remembering it as a family project that "we all enjoyed." After they were recruited, Isley recalled that her "sons opened up to talk freely" and that during such activities "we were the most together as a family." Because of such activities "we were better parents."

She contrasted such complex activities with "silly" kinds of leisure pastimes (TV and video games) which, together with modern jobs, take all the time from family activities.

George Howard wrote that "the six-hour shift let Dad be with four boys at ages when that was important."

The Kellogg's workers often spoke of the shorter hours as a moral act, stressing their willingness to share their good fortune with others. In plant-wide votes taken in the 1930's and '40's, they voted three to one for a six-hour shift. A survey in the 1940's indicated that there was a strengthening of traditional institutions that thrive when people have free time: amateur sports, clubs, churches, and community service.

While the Kellogg plant went to three eight-hour shifts in the early days of World War II (in compliance with Franklin Roosevelt's executive order mandating a longer work week), management promised workers they could return to the six-hour day as soon as the war ended. After the war, management offered generous financial incentives in an attempt to convince workers to continue the expanded eight-hour shift; but they voted three to one in 1945, and again in 1946, to return to the short shift. "I need the extra money," many workers explained, "but I need the time at home more."

According to Hunnicutt, the tide began to turn as consumerism took hold in the 1960's. A new generation of workers no longer used words like *freedom* and *family* to describe the benefits of work. They insisted that—in light of all they wanted to buy—money was now the only real job benefit, and that they could never get "enough" unless they could work full-time. Shorter hours for less money was increasingly seen as "stupid," "silly," "wasted," and only for the "weak girls," "lazy, sissy men," or "housewives" who really didn't need to work.

Finally, in the 1960's and 1970's mass amusements—notably television—began their domination of leisure time. Passive culture consumption began to replace traditional activities. Time for family, loved ones, and community activities was no longer perceived as being as valuable as what one could buy with money. On December 11, 1984, workers voted to return to the longer, eight-hour shift. W. K. Kellogg's bold and creative experiment had come to an end.

Altar

What do we place on the altar of our life? It is useful to have a visual reminder of what we hold sacred, those people and things that sustain us. Throughout the world in Christian, Jewish, Hindu, Muslim, and Buddhist homes there are altars of innumerable kinds, laden with candles, flowers, incense, photographs, statues, scripture—each in their own way honoring what is sacred, beautiful, indispensable to the spiritual strength of the family of the earth. We go to them for nourishment, for courage, to remember what we love, and who we are.

Jack and Maryanne have a family altar, around which they sit with their children one evening a week. Each brings something to share and speak about.

Elaine lost two husbands—the first in Vietnam, the second to cancer. Now, alone but very courageous, there is a deep pool of strength and wisdom in her, lessons from her grief. Several days a week she turns off the phone, lights a candle on a small altar, and simply sits quietly. She prays, she gathers pictures. She may go for a walk, and when she walks, she says, she often sings.

Create a space for an altar, nothing elaborate. It can be a small table, even a box with a colorful cloth. Sit quietly, perhaps in meditation, for a few moments, and imagine what belongs there. Allow images to arise, people, sacred objects, things that hold meaning or great love. Then place these things, one at a time, on the altar, noting how you feel to see them so honored. You may want to light a candle, say a prayer. Let this be a place you come to, a Sabbath in your home, whenever you need to remember something precious you have forgotten.

WHY TIME IS NOT MONEY

Consider the lilies of the field, how they grow;
they neither toil nor spin; and yet I say to you
that even Solomon in all his glory
was not arrayed as one of these.

— MATTHEW 6:28–29

During World War II, Britain was desperate to find a way to keep track of the resources necessary to fight the war. Economists developed a method whereby they could record and combine the value of all goods and services bought and sold each year, and use this figure to calculate the overall wealth of the nation.

With the war finally over, the newly formed United Nations decided the British model would be a useful tool for understanding and comparing the relative wealth of the nations of the world. If the number of goods and services bought and sold increased, it would indicate a solid, robust economy. If they found there was a decrease in the manufacture, production, and sale of goods, it would indicate the strength of the nation was in decline. An expanding economy was seen as a good and necessary thing for the healthy survival of the country; a declining economy was an alarming indicator that the nation's well-being was in danger. The U.N. urged its members to adopt this method as the worldwide standard, and today, all countries use this measurement—called the Gross Domestic Product, or G.D.P.— to calculate their nation's wealth.

At first glance, this simple accounting method seems a useful, reasonable, and relatively neutral tool. Upon closer inspection, however, we quickly see it is both astonishingly myopic, and insidiously dangerous—even violent—in its application. For when wealth is measured only in terms of goods and services bought and sold, only those actions involving money are seen as good and useful. Anything done in time is seen as useless.

Consider a woman in Somalia who rises early to walk two miles to the nearest well to get water for her family, returns to feed her children and ready them for school, spends the morning working the soil of the family garden, the afternoon tending to the sick and infirm of her village, then in the evening cooks and mends clothing and sings songs to her tired children and makes love with her husband. As measured by the G.D.P., this woman has no value. She is useless; a drain on the nation's wealth.

Now let us look at her cousin, who was lucky enough to go to military school and became a soldier. As a government-employed pilot, let us say he is ordered to bomb a mountain enclave deemed sympathetic to some rebel cause. In this case, a great deal of money must be spent to bury all the dead men, women, and children, to rebuild the destroyed buildings, to pay soldiers to police the area, fly in emergency personnel, hire extra doctors, and recruit foreign aid—not to mention the money needed for fuel, bombs, and military aircraft. By murdering innocent children, our young pilot has done a very good thing; he has provided an enthusiastic boost to the economy. The woman who draws water and tends the sick and feeds the children has, according to our official measurement of growth and wealth, provided nothing at all. At the end of the day, it is the pilot, not the mother, who will get the medal for service to the nation.

This horrific paradox is the very foundation of the world's official economic policy. It is repeated a billion times a day, everywhere on earth. Actions performed with love are dismissed, while actions performed with money are honored and rewarded.

What is the true measure of the wealth of a people? The creation and preservation of beauty? A strong and healthy citizenry? An educated and compassionate leadership, ensuring justice for all? A palpable sense of civic joy? A collective sense that serving our neighbor is our highest civic good? Sadly, none of these rises to the top of our list. By current standards, the Holy Grail on the altar of civilization is the health of the economy, measured by the G.D.P. Economic growth is the measure of a life well lived, a nation well run, a civilization well built.

Medical science has a very specific name to describe unrestricted cell growth in the human body: cancer. Just as undifferentiated cell growth is medically toxic, so is unrestricted economic growth ethically toxic. When we measure only the manufacture and sale of goods and services—regardless of the uses to which those goods are put, and regardless of the quality of the days and lives of the people using them—we create an economy unintentionally skewed toward military expansion, war, destruction, and other profitable and expensive endeavors. Waste, stupidity, and evil all cost money, and are, by extension, economic goods; each feeds the machine of growth.

Today we are relearning to assign economic value to parks, endangered species, air and water quality, and even solitude and sunsets. We estimate the ratio of benefits to costs when we build roads and parks and reservoirs. But these "nonmarket" values are not reflected in overall measures of the national wealth. In fact, G.D.P. rises if we replace a park with a factory, and it rises even more if the factory happens to pollute the environment. Paying for the cleanup adds yet another monetary benefit to our total.

What have we done? How have we so disordered the value and meaning of human endeavor? My friends Ben and Carolyn visit the New Mexico State Penitentiary on Sunday evenings, where they lead a Bible study and discussion among the inmates about their lives, their decisions, their actions, and the consequences of those actions. It is a rich and fertile communion, punctuated with prayer and reflection, yet in the eyes of the G.D.P. it is a waste of time. How then do we understand the value of such a ministry?

And what of Pat and Dottie and the other parents in Espanola, New Mexico, who volunteered countless hours, and the teachers who taught for free, all to create an after-school gymnastics program so the children would have positive experiences, time with their parents, and learn physical and emotional confidence? What of my friend Cora, who serves meals to the homeless? Or Cornelia, who loves to weave, and who donates her looms and her time to teach this disappearing art to young women in northern New Mexico? What of Max and David Cordova, who last winter organized a drive to provide firewood for poor families, out of the simple motivation that it needed to be done? How do we value these simple acts of kindness? This is what the official statistics will show: Nothing. Nothing noteworthy, nothing of any value was achieved through these actions.

Yet every time someone gets cancer, the G.D.P. goes up. Every time an infant dies, the G.D.P. rises. A drive-by shooting improves the economy by $20,750. If the victim dies, and there is a murder trial, the benefit to the economy leaps to well over $100,000. An oil tanker spill can contribute between five and twenty million dollars of "growth"; the benefits of an airline crash or terrorist bombing can be far greater. And consider the value gained from trade with countries our own State Department has cited for torturing their citizens. In 1995 alone, this boon added an estimated $400 billion to our national worth. And so it goes: Land mines, civil wars, church burnings—each provides a boost to our bountiful economy.

In short, we have converted destruction into an economic good. But anything that grows without money changing hands—parents who care for their children, people who voluntarily care for the sick, the dying, or the homeless, people who pray or meditate or walk in the woods—these, at best, have no value. At worst, they take away precious time and energy that could be used to grow the G.D.P.

Who would make such choices consciously? Yet they have become part of our collective belief system, encoded everywhere, and we cannot help but participate in a society governed by these preferences.

My friend Janie was visiting the home of an old potter at Santa Clara pueblo. She was admiring the enormous collection of pots her host had on display throughout his home. "How many do you have?" my friend innocently inquired. Her host lowered his eyes. "We do not count such things," he replied quietly.

During Sabbath we stop counting. How do we count friendship or laughter? How do we count the value of honesty, or bread from the oven? How can we count the sunrise, the trusting clasp of a child's hand, a melody, a tear, a lover's touch? So many truly precious things grow only in the soil of time; and we can only begin to know their value when we stop counting.

During Sabbath, things that grow in time are honored at least as much as those things we would buy and sell. At rest, we can take deeper measure of our true wealth. If we do not rest, if we do not taste and eat and serve and teach and pray and give thanks and do all those things that grow only in time, we will become more impoverished than we will ever know.

Reciting Our Precepts

One must begin in one's own life the private solutions that can only in turn become public solutions.

During the Buddhist Sabbath, lay people and monks gather to recite the precepts that govern their practice. There are hundreds of these precepts for monks, concerning everything from how you meditate to how you eat your food and how you wash your bowl. But more than the specific precepts, it is a time to reiterate what is ultimately important, sacred. Whether the Eightfold Path of Buddhism, the Five Pillars of Islam, or the Ten Commandments, most religions consider certain precepts to be guiding lights to help us find our way through darker times.

The fundamental precepts by which we guide our life are cultivated, nourished, and harvested in time. It is useful during Sabbath to clarify or reaffirm those principles that calibrate our inner compass to illuminate our inner direction.

—WENDELL BERRY

What are some of the inviolable precepts that guide your life? To be kind? To be grateful? To be honest? To serve your neighbor, to help the earth, to love children? Make a list of principles that shape your days. Include both those you currently follow and those you would like to be able to follow. On Sabbath, take time to speak them aloud, alone or with loved ones. Notice how you feel when you hear them. What resistance, what relief arises? Notice how the memory of these spoken precepts resonates in your body through the day.

A DEEPER WEALTH

All the goods of this world . . . are finite
and limited and radically incapable
of satisfying the desire that
perpetually burns within us
for an infinite and perfect good.

— SIMONE WEIL

We reward our captains of industry, our real estate tycoons and investment wizards with outrageous wealth and success. At the same time, people who work with those precious things that grow only in time—caring for children, making peace in troubled communities, harvesting the crops that feed us—these people are invisible, necessary but easily replaced, "a dime a dozen." If they were smarter, luckier, more motivated, they could be out there making real money.

And so we pay our teachers and counselors and child-care workers and farm workers a minimum daily wage, just enough to keep them alive and doing their job. But those who watch over our money, who build our computers and hotels and cars and make our movies and television programs—these people we pay five times, ten times, a thousand times as much.

This economic perversity slowly corrodes the fabric of the human family. How do we truly honor the value of people's time? Through Bread for the Journey we seek out people in impoverished communities who measure their wealth in terms of the time they have to give to their community. We never need to look very hard, for these quiet saints can be easily found in every neighborhood, city, and village.

In rural Alabama we found a small, dedicated group of volunteers serving poor, abused women and their children. They wanted to use their time to bring healing to a community touched by pain, fear, and grief. They only lacked a small amount of money. With a thousand-dollar grant from the Birmingham chapter they were able to build a food pantry, a clothing bank, and start a GED program in a small local church.

In Hard Rock, Arizona, there had been a rash of suicides and violence among young people. Local teachers and parents in this isolated community decided to start a lending library with books on psychology, self-esteem, and problem-solving for young people. The general store donated space to house and run it. Fifty dollars from the Flagstaff chapter bought a hundred and fifty books at local book and garage sales, and the "library" is already a popular retreat for local teens.

In Santa Fe, a group of fly-fishers decided to start a mentoring program, offering girls and boys from the Big Brother/Big Sister waiting list an opportunity to go fishing. There, the volunteers teach them patience, and respect, and a love of nature. Fifteen hundred dollars from the Santa Fe chapter bought fly rods, fly-tying equipment, and a telephone to staff a volunteer program that now takes sixty young people into the woods for two weeks each summer.

A small amount of financial capital, when mindfully combined with a wealth of time capital, can produce true riches for families and communities. For the last ten years, we have provided small start-up grants to people who have very little money, but who have a tremendous wealth of time, passion, and creative wisdom to dedicate to the healing of their community. While they may be financially poor, they are rich in enthusiasm and devotion.

Muhammad Yunus taught as an economist in the United States for many years before he returned, in 1972, to his native Bangladesh. He found his people devastated by famine and poverty, and he organized a daring experiment. He provided small, low-interest loans to people with no money but with a great deal of time. Their only collateral was their integrity.

Much to everyone's surprise, the poorest of the poor, ninety-four percent of whom were women with no previous income, repaid their loans. And with the money they borrowed, they built houses, started small businesses, and made clothing and furniture for other villagers. In 1996 the Grameen Bank loaned out over four hundred million dollars, all in loans of three hundred dollars or less.

"We give housing loans of three hundred dollars," says Muhammad Yunus, "adequate to build a house with a tin roof, concrete columns, and a sanitary latrine. This appears to loan recipients as a royal palace—never in their lives did they think they would enter into a house with a tin roof, let alone live in one. We have given over three hundred fifty thousand housing loans. We have had no problem in getting our money back. Our recovery rate has remained over ninety-eight percent all along."

A true marriage of money and time honors the value of both. Both time and money are essential commodities for building a just and healthy world. But during Sabbath, we specifically honor those precious things—courage, creativity, wisdom, peace, kindness, and delight—that grow only in the soil of time. When we plant our seeds in that ground—when we invest our financial capital in service of those priceless human gifts—the bountiful harvest that erupts can take our breath away.

> There were times when I could not afford to sacrifice the bloom of the present moment to any work, whether of head or hands. Sometimes, in a summer morning, having taken my accustomed bath, I sat in my sunny doorway from sunrise till noon, rapt in a reverie, amidst the pines and hickories and sumachs, in undisturbed solitude and stillness, while the birds sang around. I grew in those seasons like corn in the night, and they were far better than any work of the hands would have been. They were not time subtracted from my life, but so much over and above my usual allowance.

—HENRY DAVID THOREAU

The Wealth of Companionship

MY FRIEND TERESA WRITES:

Last year was a tough one for us. Our single friend Grace was fighting cancer, and we were totally involved in her care, her decisions, and most often, her emotional health. Three women took major responsibility for coordinating and providing her care and support. It was a very draining experience, especially as it became clear to us that we were caring for a dying woman while she and her doctor still insisted that she was not, so no hospice care was available.

I was the only one of the three who had both a job and a family at home, so I snapped first. I suddenly realized that I needed spiritual support as much as Grace did, and just praying by myself wouldn't do the trick. I needed someone else there with me—I don't know why—but I didn't want to make a big deal of it. So I called an acquaintance—not a close friend but a woman from church whom I respected—and asked her if she would go somewhere and pray with me. And she did.

The two of us sat out in the woods that afternoon as I poured out a long oral prayer to God. She responded with a prayer of her own. We must have spent thirty minutes in prayer, but at the end of it I literally felt lighter. I had passed on my burden to God and let go of it. Things were a little easier after that. I don't know why it was important for someone else to be there as witness and support, but it was.

When we are lost or afraid, we can tend to isolate, to bear down and get through it, to make it on our own. Jesus says, When two or more are gathered, there I am in your midst. *When we enter into companionship with another, something larger than ourselves is born. Choose a few people whose companionship you will seek when times are difficult. Jeff, a busy corporate executive, has a "phone friend" he calls whenever he feels lost or off-center, and needs a loving voice from outside the corporate world. Even if nothing significant is said, the care and company give birth to calm and release. Resolve to seek out those you love whenever you lose your way. One of the most precious gifts we can offer is to be a place of refuge, to be Sabbath for one another.*

HAPPINESS

THE PURSUIT OF
HAPPINESS

Just to be is a blessing.
Just to live is holy.
— RABBI ABRAHAM HESCHEL

Jesus taught many things to his disciples—wisdom, courage, faithfulness, and more—but he most certainly wanted them to be happy. *Ask, and you shall receive, that your joy may be full. . . . I have come that you may have life, and that abundantly . . . . These things I have spoken to you, that my joy may be in you, and that your joy may be full.*

Similarly, the Buddha taught his disciples to "live in joy." The King of Kosala once remarked that the Buddha's disciples seemed exceptionally jubilant, unencumbered by the grave seriousness of the more ascetic practitioners. The Buddha replied that happiness *was* the spiritual life. He frequently offered this blessing of loving-kindness: "May you be happy."

Sasaki Roshi wrote this short poem about his life:

> As a butterfly lost in a flower,
> As a bird settled on a tree,
> As a child fondling mother's breast,
> For sixty-seven years of this world,
> I have played with God.

In more secular realms, philosophers from Aristotle to Jefferson have assumed "the pursuit of happiness" was a noble aspiration of civilized life. In our own age, while we accept there may be different approaches to achieving happiness, we agree that happiness and joy are precious fruits of a life well lived. Finding happiness in life is universally perceived as an essential human endeavor. Spiritual teachers and philosophers seem to agree on this point: Life should not just make us tired; life should make us happy.

Happiness grows only in the sweet soil of time. As our time is eaten away by speed and overwork, we are less available to be surprised by joy, a sunset, a kind word, an unplanned game of tag with a child, a warm loaf of bread from the oven. But for all our striving and accomplishment, our underlying need for happiness does not withdraw and disappear. So we pursue happiness on the run, trying to make our lives more and more efficient, squeezing every task into tighter increments, hoping to somehow "get" our happiness when we are able to fit it in.

When our happiness fails to appear—when we are tired, weary, and spent—we turn to the marketplace for help. There, we are offered something that looks very much like happiness—a tantalizing substitute for happiness—something more easily acquired, more quickly and conveniently bought and sold. We are offered the satisfaction of desire.

At first blush, the satisfaction of desire seems very much

like happiness. After all, what could possibly make us happier than acquiring what we want? But if we look closely at the dynamics of desire, we quickly discover that it is a temporary and ultimately unsatisfying impulse.

The Buddha taught that desire gives birth to suffering. He said that our thirst—or "craving"—for what we desire actually causes us great sorrow. If we are always seeking for what we do not have, he said, we will always be disappointed.

The Buddha taught that there are many kinds of suffering. We can all recognize the obvious suffering of physical pain, grief, illness, and death. But he said we may be slower to identify the subtle sufferings that plague us daily: anxiety, frustration, restlessness, lack of fulfillment, not getting what we want, getting what we don't want, and having what we like taken away from us.

LAMA TASHI NAMGYAL:

We've just bought a new car and we are so happy to be in it and drive around. It's so clean, and smells so fresh, and the engine works so perfectly, and the doors and windows open and shut like silk. And then someone spills their milkshake on our front seat and we suffer. Or someone scratches the brand-new paint job in the parking lot, and we suffer. Or we have an accident and the car is totaled, and we suffer. This is the suffering of change.

We could easily embellish Lama Tashi's story. For example, when we have finally acquired one car, it is not long before we feel a need for two. When we have a small home, we are soon unhappy it is not larger. When we make $15,000 we want to make $30,000, and when we get that, we want more. Jack is a millionaire with a lovely home in a beautiful neighborhood. Yet every time I see him, he tells me how expensive everything is, and complains he doesn't have enough money. The mind never tires of generating wants and desires.

The Buddhists call this driving force *tanha*—literally, thirsting, craving, or longing. *Tanha* includes not only desire for, and attachment to, material wealth and power, but also desire for, and attachment to, people, experiences, ideas, opinions, and even spiritual accomplishments. According to the Buddha, all the trouble and strife in the world—from individual sorrows and petty personal quarrels to great wars between nations and countries—arise out of this thirst. "The world," said the Buddha, "is enslaved to thirst."

The more hurried and rushed we are, the more we are willing to trade happiness for desire—and, over time, the less we are able to discern the difference between the two. The marketplace presents us with an awesome array of choices, all designed to satisfy our hunger, choices that grow exponentially and yet never fast enough—products, services, entertainment, technology, all providing stimulus, diversion, and information. But little or any of it brings us true, lasting happiness.

Tibetan Buddhists personify this endless craving as a character they call the "hungry ghost." The hungry ghost has an enormous belly, but a very small throat. It can never consume enough to satisfy its appetite; it is always hungry, always suffering. While the marketplace insists that happiness will come when all our desires are finally satisfied, we have, in fact, built a "hungry ghost" economy. We are not creating happiness. We are producing suffering.

During Sabbath we disengage from what Abraham Heschel calls "the nervousness and fury of acquisitiveness." We surrender, for a time, our relentless desires. We will not be like the hungry ghosts. The antidote to craving is rest; we quench our thirst with Sabbath tranquillity. We invite a time in which we can taste what we have been given, take delight in what we already have, and see that it is good. We focus less on our lack, and more on our abundance. As we do, our thirst and hunger for more than we need begins to fall away. In quiet stillness we can identify our genuine needs with more precision, and separate them more easily from our mindless wants and desires. We can feel the difference between happiness—which is often simple and easy, an inner shift toward appreciation and gratefulness for what is before us—and desire, which is often frantic and relentless, cutting the heart with its sharp and painful demands.

If we do not disengage, if we stay on the wheel of desire, if we do not stop and pray and sing and walk, the pattern of our addictive craving is free to escalate without limit, until we inadvertently create a life of terrible suffering for ourselves and those we love.

Gratefulness

If the angel
deigns to come
it will be because
you have convinced
her, not by tears
but by your humble
resolve to be always
beginning; to be
a beginner.

—RAINER MARIA RILKE

Meister Eckhart, the Christian mystic, asserted that if the only prayer we ever prayed our whole life was "Thank you," that would be enough. Gratefulness cultivates a visceral experience of having enough. When we are mindful of what we have, and give thanks for the many gifts we have overlooked or forgotten, our sense of wealth cannot help but expand, and we soon achieve a sense of sufficiency we so desire. Practice thanksgiving before meals, upon rising, when going to sleep. Friends, family, food, color, fragrance, the earth, life itself—these are all gifts, perfectly gratuitous. How can we not give thanks? During Sabbath time we are less concerned with what is missing, focusing instead on sharing our gratefulness for what has already been given.

THE GOSPEL OF CONSUMPTION

You want it. You want it bad. Sometimes so much it hurts. You can taste it. You feel like you would do anything to get it. Go further than they'd suspect. Twist your soul and crush what's in your way. Then you get it. And something happens. You become the object of your desire. And it feels incredible.

—ADVERTISEMENT FOR PERFUME,
IN MACY'S WINDOW

Writing in the mid-1920's, during a time of great economic expansion, industrialist Walter Henderson Grimes lamented that it was "perfectly clear that the middle-class American already buys more than he needs." Grimes was sounding an alarm; he foresaw that the American citizen (not yet a "consumer"), with a long, proud history of self-sufficiency and support from family and neighbors, was in danger of becoming satisfied. Soon, men and women, having worked hard and long in field and garden and factory and kitchen to obtain food, clothing, and shelter, would realize they had just about all they really needed. They would realize that they could now rest together, happy and satisfied, with their good and peaceful lives. Horrified at this prospect, Grimes cautioned that "unless we have a greater outlet for our goods . . . as manufacturing efficiency increases, there will be larger groups with too much leisure."

Leisure, of course, does not produce economic expansion. And so economic cheerleaders like industrial relations counselor E. S. Cowdrick called for what he dubbed the "new economic gospel of consumption." But this new "gospel of consumption" met with some resistance, as most workers did not seem to desire new goods and services—automobiles, appliances, and amusements—as spontaneously as they did the old ones—food, clothing, and shelter. And so, it took the dedicated efforts of investors, marketing experts, advertisers, and business leaders—as well as the conspicuous and widely publicized spending examples set by the rich—to fuel the drive to increased consumption.

With this strategic shift, the business community broke its historical concentration on increasing production—whereby great technologies would free men and women from the sweat and toil of their labors—and replaced it with a completely new and improved vision of progress: *the Gospel of Mass Consumption*. This, in turn, gave birth to a new and improved advertising industry.

Thus, intentionally or not, the free marketplace canonized grasping, consumption, and desire as the essential human impulses that would drive the machine of civilization. When people spend money on things they do not need, this is good for the economy. If we are encouraged to fulfill all our desires without regulation or limitation, then the economy will benefit. All boats will rise with the tide, and everyone will get more and more of what they want. Although this new gospel of consumption and acquisition met with some understandable hesitation and disbelief in the 1930's (when we tasted the bitter fruit of a free market gone awry), when a generation of young people came home from war, we were ready to accept the new gospel. We repented, we believed, and it blessed us with its bounteous reward.

Americans now consume twice as many goods and services, per person, than we did in 1945. We buy twice as many clothes and appliances, cars, books, magazines, and telephones (not to mention our computers, televisions, home entertainment centers, fax machines, and cellular phones). We buy houses almost three times larger than the families who moved into the suburbs in the mid-1940's, and we fill them with twice as many home furnishings. We work more hours, we buy more things, and the economy prospers.

For fifty years we have proved the truth of the Gospel of Consumption. Now, just as Christians once converted the reluctant Indians, witches, and infidels, we are ready to spread the Gospel throughout the "developing" world that all wretched unbelievers may be saved. Through the propagation of a global free-market economy, we seek nothing less than the satisfaction of all the desires of all people everywhere.

Imagine this: Right now there is one automobile for every 1.7 people in the United States. A typical family of four has two automobiles. In China there is currently one automobile for every six hundred people. Imagine that within five years of being baptized into the global Gospel of Consumption, the typical Chinese family rightfully desires an automobile or two, just as the Americans have. This is reasonable, and is in fact the fundamental hope and promise of the free-market economy. But what will happen when the marketplace tries to deliver those *five hundred million* automobiles to the well-cultivated hunger of the Chinese market? There is not enough steel, petroleum, or rubber—to say nothing of clean air available to suck through the additional engines—to sustain even this relatively tiny increase in consumption. So who will be asked to give up their desires first? And who gets to decide? The endless expansion of desire, as the Buddha noted over 2500 years ago, is a fatal, impossible folly.

To want more and more, to grasp and desire and need ever-increasing amounts of goods and services, is neither a virtue nor a road to happiness, as our economic cheerleaders would have us believe. It is simply an insidious quality of the mind to desire what it does not have. Nevertheless, this has become our Gospel, our vision of Eden. And just as Eve was forbidden to taste the fruit of the Tree of Knowledge, we are forbidden one thing: We must never, ever taste the fruit of the Tree of Happiness.

Happiness is the single commodity not produced by the free-market economy. Worse than that, when we are happy, we don't feel the need to buy anything. The Sabbath, a day of delight, a day to be at peace with all we have, is a radical, dangerous prescription. Because happy people will grind the wheels of progress to a terrible halt; a bloodless revolution, without a single shot being fired.

Happiness for Free

Nasrudin used to stand in the street on market-days, to be pointed out as an idiot. No matter how often people offered him a large and a small coin, he always chose the smaller piece.

One day a kindly man said to him, "Mulla, you should take the bigger coin. Then you will have more money and people will no longer be able to make a laughingstock of you."

"That might be true," said Nasrudin, "but if I always take the larger, people will stop offering me money to prove that I am more idiotic than they are. Then I would have no money at all."

Take an hour to visit a favorite store, one where you particularly enjoy shopping. Perhaps they have many beautiful things you love, or things you would like to have if you could afford them. But today resolve to enter the store and spend a full hour shopping—knowing that you will not spend a single penny. Look at the merchandise, let yourself feel the tug of buying. Listen to the voices that speak to you: Buy me. You need me. Take me home with you. You would be so happy if you had me. *Be aware of any struggles or discomforts that arise; also be aware of any spaciousness that may arise as you let each item go, walking away, free of the impulse to acquire it—at least for today. What do you notice about your mood, your sense of sufficiency, as you leave the store at the end of this practice?*

SELLING UNHAPPINESS

In pursuit of knowledge,
  every day something is acquired.
In pursuit of wisdom,
  every day something is dropped.

—LAO TZU

We all receive catalogues in the mail with pictures of young, sophisticated women and men lounging about in natural cotton clothing, loose and soft on their sculpted bodies. It seems to be late afternoon in their Victorian house; maybe they are lovers, maybe they are having tea, one hand on the golden retriever asleep at their side. A picture of perfect happiness.

It is a picture, of course, of Sabbath time. You can taste the tea, smell the flowers on the breeze, feel the gentle support of an easy chair and the soothing company of a loving dog. The job is miles away, the factory is closed; someone else is handling things. They seem to be inviting us to join them, to become part of their lives. This, they seem to say, is how we were meant to be. Why not join us?

What they offer is the happiness of being young, at ease, perfect. Order this blouse, this cologne, this lingerie, this coffee maker, this bathrobe, this table setting, this rocking chair, and you will enter this picture. Troubles will dissolve, and life will be sweet. In the end they are selling this, and always this: Buy what we have, and you will be happy.

But beneath the text, we hear the real message: Until and unless you buy what we are selling, *you will never be happy.* Look at the people in the picture, aren't they happy? Look at the people wearing our clothes, drinking our coffee, sitting on our furniture. Don't they look happy? *We know you are not that happy.* We know that when you look at all the fun these young beautiful people are having, you will realize that *you have never been that happy.* If you ever want to be that happy, you had better buy from us while you have the chance.

A thousand times a day, in a million forms, calling to us from billboards, magazines, television, radio, newspapers, movies, Web sites, and telemarketers, every single message without exception is this: You are not enough. You do not have enough. You are not happy. You have not achieved the American Dream. Not "You are the light of the world." Not "Together we can make the world a better place." Not "Do unto others as you would have them do unto you." But rather, "You are not happy." Look, listen, and see if this is not true.

If you want to be happy, you have to drive around in a very expensive car and you have to live in a Victorian mansion so large that you have to walk through an acre of perfect gardens just to get to breakfast with your perfect children who are always laughing in your perfect kitchen and then go off in your perfect clothes to lunch and opening nights and cocktail parties with everyone else who is young and beautiful and smiling with clean, white teeth, natural clothing, and the sleeping golden retriever.

But at the same time, you know that you are not going to lead that life. It is highly improbable for most people in America, and impossible for almost everyone else in the world. How does that make you feel? Sad, inadequate, unhappy? That is what you are supposed to feel. That is what they are selling, and that is what we are buying: our own unhappiness.

When you see movie stars and sports heroes and television personalities and all the beautiful models and wealthy people doing beautiful, exciting, happy things, they are always presented as the way we, too, would live if we were happy and successful. We would live like that, too, if we were ever successful. But we do not live like them. We do not look like them. And no matter how hard we work and how much money we spend buying the things they have, we will never really be like them. Those pictures are a fiction. They are a lie.

For when we get the clothing, the coffee maker, the furniture, the perfume, it comes in the mail, it comes to our house, into our own weary and hurried life. We are too tired from working to wear it, drink it, sit in it, or enjoy it. The package is delivered to our life, our world—not theirs. Now we have to work even harder to pay for something we did not need and did not even really want—except that we wanted the peace, the sunset, the lover, the quiet, the rest. Now we have nothing except another bill to pay.

The lie is this: While they are promising happiness, they are really selling dissatisfaction. Our entire economy is predicated upon dissatisfaction. If we are satisfied, we do not need more than we already have. Once we have eaten our fill, we do not ask for another helping. If we are happy in our marriage, we are not desperate to have an affair. If we are satisfied with our home and our community, we will feel no desire to move. When we are happy, we are not driven to grasp for more than we have.

Some of us seek relief from our dissatisfaction by turning to more spiritual pursuits. But time is the country in which all spiritual practices live and breathe. To pray, to meditate, to cultivate mindfulness, compassion, and care requires time and attention. If we have not stopped long enough to sow and cultivate these seeds, a fruitful spiritual practice will be very difficult indeed.

So the marketplace, sensing our desire for things spiritual, offers to sell them to us. Simply buy this new self-help book, this yoga video, these Zen gardening tools, these crystals, bells, incense, statues, cushions—then you will be spiritual and self-aware. Then you will be holy, healed, and happy. After a while we add "spirituality" to our growing list of desires for good food, fine clothing, and a new refrigerator. Our hungry ghosts find no rest.

It is imperative that we recognize that our particular model of civilization is actually *designed to produce suffering*. If we simply work harder and longer and more efficiently to make it work better—without stopping to see what we have built—*we will simply produce suffering more efficiently*.

Sabbath is a time to stop, to refrain from being seduced by our desires. To stop working, stop making money, stop spending money. See what you have. Look around. Listen to your life. Do you really need more than this? Spend a day with your family. Instead of buying the new coffee maker, make coffee in the old one and sit with your spouse on the couch, hang out—do what they do in the picture without paying for it. Just stop. That is, after all, what they are selling in the picture: people who have stopped. You cannot buy stopped. You simply have to stop.

Spend a day napping and eating what is left over in the refrigerator; play a game with your children, take a walk, have a cup of tea, make love, do nothing of any consequence or importance. Then, at the end of the day, where is the desperate yearning to consume, to shop, to buy what we do not need? It dissolves. Little by little, it falls away.

PRACTICE:

Morning Rituals

Only one hour in the normal day is more pleasurable than the hour spent in bed with a book before going to sleep, and that is the hour spent in bed with a book after being called in the morning.

— ROSE MACAULAY

My dear friend Doug Wilson has developed a potent new spiritual practice. He calls it "Slotha Yoga." It consists of one simple precept: When you wake up, don't get up. Stay in bed. Give yourself time to review your dreams. Notice how it feels to be in your body this morning. Do not be hurried by your impending responsibilities, but rather luxuriate in the softness of the bedcovers. Watch how the light is coming into the room today, read a little, day-dream, wonder about breakfast.

Many couples begin their Sabbath morning in this way. Peter and Anne let their older children know not to disturb them on Saturday morning. They wake slowly, and over time, begin to share their thoughts about the week, linger-ing feelings, meanderings of the soul only spoken between lovers when there is time. "This," Anne tells me, "almost always leads to lovemaking, which is such a precious part of Sabbath for us."

My friends Ken and Carol, their children grown and moved away, always have champagne in bed on Sabbath mornings, where they play their sacred weekly game of Scrabble. They have kept this ritual for years, and friends know not to violate that time.

The fruitful uselessness of rest, play, and delight can begin on a Sabbath morning. Wake up, but do not get up. Do something delightful. Use your imagination, be frivolous, be daring. Invent rituals. Do nothing of any significance. Cultivate expertise in Slotha Yoga.

THE TYRANNY OF CHOICE

Suppose that a warrior forgot that he was already
wearing his pearl on his forehead, and sought for
it somewhere else; he might search through the
whole world without finding it. But if someone
simply pointed it out to him, the warrior would
immediately realize that the pearl had been there all
the time.

— HUANG PO

When we lived in Santa Fe, in the yard behind our
home there was a rich diversity of life forms that
shared a small plot of high desert soil. There was a
patch of grass in the center, ringed by a few fruit trees,
hollyhocks, lilies, daffodils, irises, and poppies, each
coming up in their own time and place. There was
tarragon, cilantro, rosemary, and sage; there was lilac,
aspen, and golden locust. I planted each one, new
things each year, depending on which color or fragrance seemed to call out for balance. Without any
effort of mine came the magpies, crows, and blue jays;

rattlesnakes, bull snakes, centipedes, and tarantulas; lizards, hummingbirds, and, of course, the gophers. Gophers that tunneled everywhere and ate everything (except, miraculously, the daffodils). They were particularly fond of the roots of fruit trees. I had a peach tree that, after eight years of attentive watering, fertilizing, and pruning, was several feet shorter than when I planted it.

And then there were the tulips. I recall my astonishment when, as a novice gardener, I first learned the miracle of perennials. Imagine putting a bulb in the ground one year, and having the flowers come back faithfully, year after year, without ever having to plant them again. It instantly deepened my respect and admiration for the immeasurable cleverness of the Creator.

Armed with this revelation, I pored through bulb catalogues and ordered a colorful mixture that I planted, in the fall, around the birdbath and in a small patch in front of the house. All winter I waited, looking forward to the sea of tulips that would arrive in the spring, just like the picture in the Smith and Hawken catalogue.

Sure enough, in April, a beautiful pattern of green pointed leaves peeked out through the cold ground. Two days later, they were all gone. They had been eaten down to stubs, each and every one. I was crushed. The next two years the same thing happened. The bulbs managed to push up about an inch of leaves, and then they would disappear back into the ground.

I had discovered a critical factor in the growth and cultivation of perennials that was not mentioned in the Smith and Hawken catalogue: jackrabbits. Jackrabbits abound in the Southwest, and for the first three years I accepted their eating the tulips as my gift to them; all beings were getting some benefit from our garden, I told myself. Then I decided to build a fence.

The people at our local nursery told me that a small, ten-inch-high fence around the tulips would be enough to discourage the jackrabbits. Even though they could easily jump over it if they tried, it would be enough to deter their curiosity. They would simply eat the abundant grasses and weeds instead.

Sometimes it is necessary to stop one thing before another thing can begin. The following year, I saw for the first time the reds and purples I had only imagined. The fence was a simple prohibition against harmful activity. As soon as the harmful activity was prevented, something in the ground, waiting patiently to be born, could grow.

The traditional thirty-nine prohibitions against working on the Jewish Sabbath gave birth to what one scholar calls "the most precious, inestimable pearl" of Sabbath tranquillity. Similarly, most of the Ten Commandments begin with "Thou shalt not." These prohibitions against stealing, lying, murdering, and the like, if practiced with a fullness of heart, set us free to turn our energies to other things more precious—to honesty, fidelity, generosity, and love.

But progress promises us the endless expansion of choice; we chafe at any restriction on our capacity to generate options, and we revolt against any concept of prohibition. Why should we not be allowed to cook, clean, build, buy, sell, write, plow, or harvest whenever we feel like it? Who do these ancient sages think they are anyway, always telling us what we are not allowed to do?

But what if we hear these prohibitions with different ears? What if, like the fence around my tulips, these teachings are not the punitive restrictions of a grumpy, humorless parent—"You are not allowed to do these things because we say so, and that's all you need to know about that"—but rather a useful boundary that keeps out those things that would bring us harm? Time and again, in spiritual practice, we are asked to imagine that certain limitations on our choices are actually seeds of great freedom.

We equate choice with freedom, but they are not the same. If we exercise our choice to covet or to steal or to live without rest, we will soon feel trapped and unhappy. We equate choice with nourishment, but a dozen different soft drinks, potato chips, and candy bars provide no vitamin C, iron, protein, beta carotene—or any significant nutrition at all. Regardless of how many choices we pile one upon the other, it is still a big, fat, empty meal.

And what of the burgeoning choices in the ways we communicate? Have express mail, telephone, cell phone, fax, e-mail, the World Wide Web given us more freedom? In fact, the more our choices multiply, the more we feel trapped, overwhelmed, and overburdened by the sheer weight of communication coming at us from every direction. We end up feeling imprisoned and paralyzed, not free at all.

Freedom of choice can be as painful as it is precious. We want to be able to choose whatever career, spouse, or neighborhood we wish, but how do we decide, what should we look for, should we go to school now or later, have children now or later, stay home with the children and risk getting passed over by more aggressive colleagues, or push a career now and hope that day care is a nurturing option? How do we decide which partner we love, whether to change our neighborhood or political party, or start exploring new spiritual traditions?

Freedom of choice can suffocate us; we drown in a sea of options. Every act must be thoroughly deliberated, weighed against all other options, researched, agonized over, responded to, and figured out before we can feel absolutely right about any choice at all. Even when we finally make our choice, we wrestle with guilt, uncertainty, and fear: With so much else we could have chosen, how do we ever know we have done the right thing?

The Sabbath is a patch of ground secured by a tiny fence, when we withdraw from the endless choices afforded us and listen, uncover what is ultimately important, remember what is quietly sacred. Sabbath restrictions on work and activity actually create a space of great freedom; without these self-imposed restrictions, we may never be truly free.

Sister Gilchrist is a Cistercian nun at the Abbey of the Mississippi. She is a bright, dynamic woman with a sharp mind and a kind heart. Like many nuns, she has a variety of responsibilities in the keeping of the abbey, which include cooking and helping manage the land on which they keep a herd of cattle. Sister Gilchrist delights in walking the fields in the afternoon, picking from the few wild herbs that grow there, and bringing them back to the kitchen to add fresh spice and fragrance to the evening supper.

A few years ago, the sisters became interested in permaculture, and sought consultation to discover the most efficient and sustainable use for both land and animals. They were advised to change the grazing habits of their cattle. Where previously the cattle roamed freely over the entire field, they were told to pen the cattle in smaller areas, to thoroughly graze—and fertilize—a small patch of land. The rest of the field could lie fallow. Later, they moved the pen to another spot, and in this way each section of land was fully used, and then allowed to rest.

After two years of this new grazing method, Sister Gilchrist went out in early spring to check on the growth of her precious herbs. To her astonishment, she found not only the few herbs she was familiar with, but over a dozen new ones that had miraculously appeared, apparently out of nowhere. Several new grasses had germinated as well, grasses that, when the cows began to graze on them, proved so nourishing that the sisters were able to stop supplementing the cows' diet with corn. The nutrition in the new grasses was more than sufficient to sustain them.

Where had these new herbs and grasses come from? They appeared from within the earth of this field, seeds that had always been embedded in the soil. Because they had always been trodden underfoot by the relentless activity of the cows, they were never able to grow into their fullness. When the land and the seeds were given a necessary Sabbath, the earth could then, in its own time, reveal the breathtaking wonders of which it was naturally and easily capable.

Stopping to Rest

Stephen is an editor at a busy publishing house in Manhattan. "I used to work eight days a week. Now I work only seven," he quips. He decided he would not take manuscripts home, no longer read them on Saturdays—something editors are routinely expected to do. But, in the beginning, he was perplexed as to what to do with his extra time. "I did not know what to do with myself," he confesses. Slowly, over time, he developed a practice of visiting the farmers' market and spending the better part of the morning choosing fresh vegetables, fruits, and flowers to bring home.

Francine, with breast cancer, writes a poem every day. Not to publish, although she is a poet. But to keep the language moving through her body, so the words and thoughts do not get stuck.

Julie has chronic fatigue, but forces herself to draw or sketch something every day, a creative pause to quicken the life force.

Choose one pleasurable activity that is easily done and takes little time. Leaf through a magazine and tear out a picture that you find appealing; put it somewhere you will see it, and notice how you respond to it throughout the day. Write a short poem about nothing of any importance. Put a new flower in a cup by your bed. Take a walk around the block. Sing a song you know from beginning to end. Do something simple and playful like this every day. Take a crayon and make a simple drawing of your bedroom. Let the power of a simple act of creativity stop you, slow your pace, interrupt your speed. Notice how willing you are to be stopped. Notice how it feels when you are.

SENSUALITY AND DELIGHT

How beautiful are your feet . . .
the curves of your thighs are like jewels . . .
your waist is a heap of wheat set about with lilies . . .
your twin breasts are like two fawns.
—SONG OF SOLOMON

Let us suppose we have surrendered to certain prohibitions, made our home a restful place, and removed ourselves from the seductive din of options and choices. We have closed the store, turned off the phone, put the car keys in a drawer, unplugged the radio and television and computer. How, then, do we begin to rest? Sabbath is supposed to be a time of delight. How do we find delight when we feel the lingering tug of so many choices, worries, and responsibilities?

The Sabbath wisely begins its work on us by engaging our physical senses as a way of quieting our mind. Sabbath time is a sensual time, a feast of pleasures and sensations. The journey from work to rest, from action to Sabbath, is first felt in the body. During Sabbath time we sing with our mouths, we pray with our hands, we light candles, we smell the spices, we eat warm bread, we touch one another as we give and receive our blessings. It is a delight for the senses.

When Hindus worship they literally feed colorfully adorned deities on the *puja*, or altar, with fruits and sweets, offering gifts of flowers, fragrances, and songs. Native American ceremonies often begin with the fragrance of burning sweet grass and sage. The Sabbath, with all its food, song, and candles is a sensual experience that reminds us we cannot fully comprehend the sweet magnificence of God in a purely intellectual way; we feel the tangible presence of spirit and creation directly with our body.

Karen grew up in a Jewish home, but as an adult she did not continue keeping the Sabbath. When she was thirty years old her sister was to be married in another state, and Karen stayed with a cousin whose husband was the cantor at the temple. "My cousin had prepared a Shabbat supper on Friday night before the wedding. Walking into her house was like entering another world. It was so warm and inviting, the chairs had soft, deep cushions, someone played piano, the smell of good, wholesome food filled the house. I felt so welcome, a deep, unexpected belonging. When we gathered around the table and my cousin lit the candles and began praying, I burst into tears. I was so uncontrollably affected by the overwhelming sensuality of it, such a warm and loving bath. I had to go into the bedroom by myself and cry for a long time before I could join them at the table. I knew then that I had to come back to this, that I belonged here, in this kind of place and time."

We use the phrase "to know in the biblical sense" as a euphemism for making love because when we truly make love we open our bodies and hearts and feel the essence of our beloved in a profoundly intimate way. There are countless metaphors across mystical traditions that invite us to make love with the divine, that personify wisdom as *Sofia,* as a beautiful woman. The Song of Solomon is an erotic love poem between a man and a woman, a sensory feast that suggests that to be one with the beloved is to surrender into the tangible pleasure of spiritual fulfillment: *Let me kiss you with the kisses of my lips, for your mouth is sweeter than wine . . . Oh, may your breasts be like clusters of the vine, and the scent of your breath like apples, and your kisses like the best wine that goes down smoothly, gliding over lips and teeth.* Kabbalists in the Israeli mountain city of Safad greet the coming of Sabbath as a groom desiring his bride. At sunset, after ritual bathing, they dress themselves in white, and walk out to the fields on the edge of town to greet her.

In Exodus, Moses encounters a burning bush, and the presence of God calls out to him, "Put off your shoes from your feet, for the place on which you are standing is holy ground." The rabbis interpret this not so much as a warning to Moses because this particular ground is holy, but rather that the shoes represent something dead or foreign between our feet and the ground on which we stand. With bare feet Moses can literally feel the holiness come up into him, with nothing separating his body from the tangible blessing of sacred ground. As Brother David Steindl-Rast explains, "Whenever we take off our shoes, we will realize that we have been standing on holy ground."

Sabbath invites us to take off our shoes, and allow our bodies to touch the earth. Fleshy tenderness meets grass, dirt, sand, and rock, cool and warm and sensual like a lover's touch, feet on ground like a kiss, an embrace. Walk slowly on a patch of ground, feel it on the feet, feel the angles, curves, irregularities, know it the way you know the body of a lover, every fold and mound and line.

At the Sebastiani winery in northern California, there is a small open room where you sit and relax before entering the winery proper. Centuries ago, such an area was used by the monks to wash their visitors' feet, in an exercise of humility and hospitality. The act of making wine is a sensual experience, from the picking and crushing of the grapes to the first sip of sweet wine. To visit such a kingdom our feet must touch fertile ground.

Every day I walk the beach by my cottage not far from that winery. My feet press into sand, lapped by cool water, the texture of rock and shell pushing into my heel, jasmine in the air, mist and color and sky and sea and salt in the air and fog, always fog, an ever-present, quietly everywhere moist and velvet prayer suspended in the ether that floats all around my skin. The fog engages in playful, delicate intercourse with the coast of northern California, and I cannot help but be quickened by it.

At the Last Supper, Jesus took off his clothes and wrapped himself in a towel, poured water over the naked feet of his friends and, one by one, taking time with each, washed their feet. Water, hands, touch, flesh, intimate sensual contact; a final act of intimacy, of knowing, before he would leave them. As if touching them, naked flesh to naked flesh, were a sanctification of his love for them.

The Talmud prescribes the Sabbath as a time for making love, to feel in our bodies the delicious union with God and our beloved, to bridge any separation we may feel from our divine nature or our natural joy. God aches for us; we respond by removing our clothing, and in our nakedness, skin receptive, open and available and vulnerable, we touch and are touched, intimately known and held. How else would we know the sweet blessings of God?

Why does the Sabbath emphasize sensuality and touch? It is a language of healing, of blessing. When premature infants are regularly massaged, they gain precious weight more easily. When mothers in labor are caressed, they become more physically loving with their children. When we lay on hands, when we place a hand on the brow of an infant and utter a prayer of baptism, when we cleave together to make life, when we break bread and eat, when we join hands in prayer, we are in deep conversation with the spirit of creation. All life arises through touch; nothing living thrives without physical contact.

Marion has a son, Michael, who is hyperactive. After trying various failed medications, she decided to use her deep love for him as her primary treatment. Whenever he began to lose control of his impulses, Marion would scoop him up and sit him in her lap, place his head against her chest, and rock, and rock, until, she said, he could remember who he was.

The Sabbath rocks us and holds us until we can remember who we are. If we are to deeply and fully integrate rest into the rhythm of our lives, we need a sense memory, a visceral bodily experience of what it feels like to be delightfully inactive. Students who study in the presence of a fragrance do better on tests when the same fragrance is later present in the testing room. On the Sabbath we smell spices, we bring flowers, we smell the bread in the oven, and we are transported, we recall feelings and insights we have known before, and we remember. When Sabbath is done and we return to our labor, we carry the fragrance of rest in our bodies.

The Sabbath prohibitions restrict those things that would impede our sensuality. Walk leisurely, don't drive; walk in the garden, don't answer the phone, turn off the television and the radio, forget the CD and the computer. Quiet the insidious technology, and remember that we live in bodies that, through a feast of the senses, appreciate the beauty of the world. Walk under the stars and moon. Knock on the door, don't ring. Sing at the table. Eat, drink, touch, smell, and remember who you are.

A day so happy.
Fog lifted early, I walked in the garden.
Hummingbirds were stopping over
      honeysuckle flowers.
There was no thing on earth I wanted to possess.
I knew no one worth envying him.
Whatever evil I had suffered, I forgot.
To think that once I was the same man
      did not embarrass me.
In my body I felt no pain.
When straightening up, I saw the blue sea and sails.

— CZESLAW MILOSZ

Take Off Your Shoes

I climb a tree, reach for a plum, and eat it, but in a moment the plum is gone and I have nothing. The sad conclusion of this way of seeing is that the search for the sacred must go on someplace else. In text and words which grow more pale the farther away they are placed from life.

But one can also say that in placing that plum in my mouth I have experienced joy. The fruit of many months of sunlight and earth and water has entered me, becomes me, not only in my stomach, my blood, my cells, but because of what I have learned. The plum has been my lover. And I have known the plum. Letting the plum into the mind of my body, I will always have that taste of sweetness in my memory.

—SUSAN GRIFFIN

Take off your shoes. Stand still and quiet for a moment. Let your feet touch earth, soil, floor, and rock. Feel the visceral holiness rise up and kiss tender, naked flesh.

Walk slowly. Let each step be a prayer, each footfall a sacred kiss of flesh and earth. Let each sensation rise up the body. Feel how the body receives the blessing of holy ground.

WISDOM

DOING GOOD BADLY

The art of medicine consists of
amusing the patient
while nature cures the disease.
—VOLTAIRE

In the late 1970's I was part of a group of people who believed in deinstitutionalization, or returning people who had been confined in juvenile homes and psychiatric hospitals back to the communities from which they came. At the time I was the chair of the Delinquency Prevention Commission in California, and we believed that status offenders—children who were truant, runaways, or convicted of minor, nonviolent offenses—would be better treated outside the criminal justice system. By giving young, nonviolent offenders a measure of respect, and freedom to learn to make decisions at an earlier age, we hoped that we would not only save money, but also fully engage the community in the raising of our children. At the same time, our colleagues in community mental health were making similar decisions about institutionalized psychiatric patients. If we returned them to their community, they would need less public money, and they would be free to be cared for by their families, back home where they belonged.

However, in neither case did we spend enough time with the communities to which these children and adults would be returned. We did not take the time to sit quietly and listen to the families from which they had come. We did not take even a Sabbath day to reflect more deeply on the eventual implications of our actions.

What would our truants and runaways need, now that they were "free"? Surely better schools, better supervision at home, more community support. Where was that going to come from? From their fractured families? Who would watch and care for these children, and how would they be provided for? Without stopping, eager to be useful, we just let them go. Now the nation is awash in lost children, some violent, many in pain. And now they are not first-time offenders, they are multiple felons. We, for our part, now rush to blame them for threatening the safety of our society, and we cannot build prisons fast enough to hold them.

And so with all the deinstitutionalized psychiatric patients. Did we go to their communities and ask who would care for them? Why did their families not care for them before? What would they need to do it better now? We were rushed, flush with our own compassion, and energized to speedily liberate all these poor unfortunate patients. Now, our former patients swell the ranks of a disjointed army of homeless women and men who sleep in gutters, shelters, church basements, on subway grates, and under bridges—anywhere but in a nice, warm bed with people to care for them.

The point is not that the impulse to care for these children and adults in our communities was not wise. Institutionalization is not necessarily beneficial for children or the mentally ill, and they may, in the long run, be better served by living in community with others. But we were in a terrible hurry to do good, and there was no rest in our decisions. And just as speech without silence creates noise, charity without rest creates suffering.

In our frenzy to make the world a better place, it is easy to presume that the romance and magic of our good intentions will protect us from doing unintended harm. For example, how many of us—touched by heart-wrenching photos of starving children in the Sahel region of equatorial Africa—mailed our donations to help the poor, unfortunate children in the early 1990's? But how many of us would be shocked to discover that our generosity had contributed to their suffering?

The nomadic peoples of the Sahel were being impoverished by the incursion of commercial farmers on traditional grazing lands. In response, the United States Agency for International Development rushed to their aid, and drilled deep wells to provide drinking water for the nomads' cattle, believing this would protect them from poverty and famine.

But there was no quiet, no rest in that decision; no sitting with these people, no listening to how the earth turned in that place. For hundreds of years there had been a delicate equanimity between the wet and dry seasons, maintaining a fragile balance among the cattle, the availability of drinking water, and the sparse grasses that grew on the dry plains. When the new wells were drilled the cattle populations exploded, the fragile lands were overgrazed, and then cattle began to die in unprecedented numbers. In the end, our good intentions helped create a terrible famine in the land.

We are driving at night, hurtling down some dark country road. Suddenly, in our headlights, we see a deer leap in front of the car. We swerve, brake, skid, perhaps hit the deer, perhaps not. We are lucky to escape unharmed.

Everything is more dangerous at high speed. Even a deer—an unexpected blessing when we come upon her while hiking in the woods—becomes an object of terror and harm. As we drive forward without stopping, even our generosity takes on the characteristics of a high-speed train, forcing compassion, wanted or not, right prescription or not, on everything unlucky enough to get in our path. Even a good heart can cause harm for ourselves and others if it has no rest in it.

Love, too, requires rest; unstructured moments of intimate companionship, seeing, touching, and being with. Our presence and attention are the tangible manifestations of true love. This is most obvious when we try to hurry our children. For children, time is the nectar of care; it cannot be concentrated into bursts of "quality time." Nor can love be postponed while we boost our current income, borrowed from the present, to be repaid at a more convenient date.

We are every day becoming aware of the costs of a life without rest. Increasingly, social workers, courts, and probation officers are raising our children, rescuing them from the unintentional wasteland of our hyperactivity. Our most valuable legacy—the wealth of the children of the earth—is starving for our time and our love. We are expected to sacrifice more of our time to work, seeking more work, being on call for work, and recovering from overwork. Then, with the money we make, we can buy more things for our children, things like televisions and computers and CD's and video games that will give them, the marketeers insist, a happy childhood.

During Sabbath we take the time to bless our children, place our hands upon their heads, our fingers in their hair, and pray for their strength, and courage, and happiness. We rest with them, eat with them, play with them, walk with them, listen to their stories and their worries and their laughter, and remember to whom they belong. All the video games and cable television and computers and clothes and CD's in the galaxy cannot place a single hand on a single head and grant this Sabbath blessing.

I have a friend who was always involved with a million projects at once. One day, exhausted and burned out, he went on a meditation retreat. For the first time, he settled deep into himself and got very quiet. He heard the incessant graspings of his mind, he watched the hurried quality of his actions. Over time, at rest at last, he began to feel a peace and well-being that welled up naturally and effortlessly within him.

He fell in love with this practice. He began meditating regularly, and derived great benefit from it. He began sharing with his friends the peace he was experiencing. Friends came to him for instruction and guidance, and he began to teach small meditation classes. These classes became so well attended that over time they evolved into a center for spirituality and meditation. Now my friend is involved with a multitude of meditation projects and centers. He offers the gift of practice with great love and enthusiasm. Yet, once again, he is busy all the time and I can rarely get him on the phone. When I do, he complains he hardly has time for meditation.

When I worked as a community organizer in the poorer Boston neighborhoods of Roxbury and Dorchester, we often had meetings with local teachers, parents, clergy, and social activists, trying again and again to listen for the healing that would be possible in the lives of the struggling families who lived there. One day we were meeting in Old South Church, one of the fine, traditional houses of worship in Boston. One social activist was particularly enthusiastic in criticizing the great disparities of wealth in the city. In his evangelical fervor, he used the church we were sitting in as an offending example. "Take this church. It is obscene, all this stained glass and gold chalices and fine tapestries. If the church really cared about poor people, they should sell all of this and give it to the poor." This argument is not new; it was made by Jesus' disciples themselves, and it clearly has some merit. But a woman from the neighborhood, who had lived there all her life, said quietly, "This is one of the most beautiful places in the city. It is one of the only places where poor folks can afford to be around beauty. All the other beauty in this city costs money. Here, we can be surrounded by beautiful things, and it all belongs to us. Don't even think about taking away what little beauty we have."

We are a nation of hectic healers, refusing to stop. Our drive to do better faster, to develop social programs more rapidly, to create helpful agencies more quickly can create a sea of frantic busyness with negligible, even questionable, results. In our passionate rush to be helpful, we miss things that are sacred, subtle, and important.

Doing good requires more than simply knowing what is wrong. Like God in the creation story, we need Sabbath time to step back, pause, and be quiet enough to recognize what is good.

Laurie had breast cancer. Her doctors told her she must have chemotherapy or she would die. But Laurie was also pregnant, and the chemotherapy could seriously damage her unborn child. If she refused chemotherapy, her child might be born healthy, but might also grow up without a mother. If Laurie chose the treatment, she could live to raise a deformed or disabled child. What should she do?

Laurie decided to pray. She prayed quietly, without words, meditating on a single, unspoken question suspended in the silence. As she prayed, she listened. She let the worries of her whole life fall away and listened to this singular question; every beat of her heart became a prayer. On the night before she was to go to the hospital and begin treatment, the last night she could refuse it, she had a dream. In the dream, she saw her child in her belly. It was alive, and surrounded by a warm and lovely light. She knew this light, and she knew it would protect her child. The next morning she began the treatments that would save her life. She became the mother of a strong and healthy baby girl.

The words *cure* and *curious* share the same root. During Sabbath, we can listen with openness and curiosity—what Buddhists call *choiceless awareness*. Here, voices can speak to us, voices we hear only in the quiet. Only at rest can we hear what we have not heard before, and be led to what is most deeply beautiful, necessary, and true.

PRACTICE:

Patience

When my friend Mark Nepo struggled with his cancer, he underwent a variety of treatments, radiation, chemotherapy, more than once. After a long and difficult period he asked the doctors to please stop. He could feel his body cry out for time, time to rest from the treatments, time to heal. Going to the hospital week after week, month after month for treatments and tests was, he said, like planting a seed in good soil, and every day pulling it up to check the roots. It cannot take hold; it withers from overexamination. Now, years later and free from cancer, he knows to allow these Sabbath moments to lie fallow, to let things be, and listen for what grows where we cannot see. But we can hear what grows when left alone, silent, invisible. He wrote this poem:

WHAT TIES ME TO THE EARTH IS UNSEEN

My heart was beating like a heron awakened
in the weeds, no room to move. Tangled
and surprised by the noise of my mind,
I fluttered without grace to the center
of the lake which humans call silence.

I guess, if you should ask, peace
is no more than the underside
of tired wings resting on the lake
while the heart in its feathers
pounds softer and softer.

Imagine a situation that concerns you. What changes in your body—tension, heartbeat, respiration—when you think of it?

163

Now imagine that it is growing toward resolution in some invisible soil. During Sabbath, we rely on forces larger than ourselves at work on healing the world. Imagine these forces at work this moment on your problem. Imagine, as a seed knows how to grow and blossom and flower, just as the body knows how to heal, this problem may already know how to be resolved. How does this change your feeling about the dilemma?

BE STILL AND KNOW

He makes me lie down in green pastures;
he leads me beside still waters.
He restores my soul.
— TWENTY-THIRD PSALM

Sabbath is an incubator for wisdom. When we allow the rush and pressure of our days to fall away, even for a short period of time, we are more able to discern the essential truth of what lies before us. Jesus said, *If the eye is simple and clear, the body will be full of light;* and, *Those that have ears, let them hear.* Through meditation, prayer, and stillness, we refine our vision, we sharpen our hearing. When I train counselors, sometimes I ask them to close their eyes and meditate while their clients are speaking. Surprisingly, they often report they can hear what their clients are trying to say *beneath the words*. Sabbath is like this, a day of closing our eyes to the busyness of our necessary responsibilities, a meditation in the midst of life, a day to listen more carefully to the story beneath the habitual words and actions that flood our days.

Dottie Montoya volunteers with Bread for the Journey. She is a public health nurse in Espanola, a poor community in northern New Mexico. For years she has worked closely with children in schools, many of whom get their primary medical care from the school nurse. Because of her love for these children, she often finds herself involved with their families as well, visiting them at home and trying to listen for the places where help is possible.

Dottie told me of a boy, Roberto, whom she first met nine months ago. He was having difficulty keeping up with the other children in the class, and was also getting into fights. Dottie suspected there were problems at home. One afternoon she went to visit his mother, Rosa, who met Dottie on the porch, carrying a belt in one hand, a beer in the other, a cigarette dangling from the corner of her mouth. Rosa was angry with her children, frustrated as a single mother living in a run-down trailer, and clearly unhappy with her life. Dottie sat with Rosa for a long time, offering the simple gift of her presence and her ear.

Because of the lack of effective local services for families in need, Dottie had begun to invite parents to help other parents with one another's children. Her informal network included many single parents who would help one another with shopping, or baby-sitting, or transportation to the doctor. Most of all, these parents were companions to one another; they did not feel so isolated and alone, and did not have to bear the tremendous weight of caring for their children without money, resources, or companionship. She asked Rosa if it would be all right if another parent from the neighborhood came over once in a while, just to help out. Rosa took a while to answer, her loneliness in deep conversation with her pride. In the end, Rosa reluctantly agreed to allow them to visit her.

Last week Dottie told me she went to visit Roberto's mother, now nine months after that first meeting. Roberto had been doing much better in school, his grades improved, with no fighting. Dottie arrived to find Rosa's yard was now clean. Flowers had been planted, and awnings put up over the windows. Rosa came out in a clean dress and asked Dottie in for tea. What had happened? Despite all the social service agencies, government assistance programs, and caseworkers brought to bear on this woman, none of them had been able to provide the simple presence required to hear the truth of what was needed. None of these well-intentioned programs were able to see with seeing eyes, or hear with hearing ears this woman's deep, crippling loneliness. The unconditional companionship of another parent was a missing catalyst needed to help Rosa reclaim her strength and dignity, which were embedded deep within her all the while, however dormant, even in the midst of her confusion and pain.

When we move too fast we shield ourselves from the actual experience of suffering; we see only its outward manifestations and appearances. In our frantic craving for relief, we try to make the appearance of suffering go away. But we risk eradicating the symptoms without ever understanding the disease. In her quiet way, simply by being present, Dottie heard Rosa's loneliness, and introduced her to other parents who were willing to keep her company.

Of course, all our social ills cannot be solved through simple presence. People need access to quality medical care, adequate housing, social and criminal justice, good jobs, and better schools. Many systemic problems require community-wide attention. But even then, without stillness, without being present, we will get it wrong. We will miss the simple, quiet opportunities for shifting the pattern. If we are still, we can hear more accurately what is truly necessary. We do not create a whirlwind of useless intervention, which sadly characterizes much of our current "social service" infrastructure. Instead, we can touch where there is an opening, a readiness, a place of grace waiting to be born—rather than forcing our prescription down the throat of some person or community that is already choking on too many prepackaged solutions.

At Bread for the Journey we do not begin with a traditional needs assessment. Human needs are limitless, and—if we are to believe the Buddha—sorrows and wants are the inevitable portion of a human life. All needs assessments lead to this same inevitable conclusion: If people are alive, they will have unmet needs.

Instead we begin with a strength assessment. Where in the community is the hidden wholeness, who are the people with courage and vision, those whose faith still burns bright and hot? Where is the wisdom, the passion? Where is the spark of the divine fire that refuses to be extinguished? When we enter into relationship with a community in need, when we sit quietly and listen, and patiently wait, a host of people with priceless gifts, talents, and strengths invariably arise. If we are to be faithful servants of the family of the earth, we must learn to listen, restfully, for the unmistakable footprint of the divine.

There is a Taoist saying: "To the mind that is still, the world surrenders." Sabbath mind is a mind that can be still, a mind that can rest in delight. A day of rest, a moment of prayer, a time of meditation, these disrupt the pattern of desperation that infects our thinking, and allow us to be able to see the healing that is already present in the problem.

God says, *My words are written in your heart.* Jesus says, *You are the light of the world.* Buddha says, *You are all Buddhas.* If these pronouncements are true, then the healing required is already present in those who seek to be healed. Healing for the poor can be found among the poor, healing for the hungry can be found among the hungry. This does not mean we should not act on their behalf—on the contrary, we must. But when we do, we act with unshakable knowing that the Sabbath principle is at work even in this: It is good.

Even in suffering, there is grace, strength, and wisdom. Doing good means uncovering and evoking the good that is already there. In the creation story, what was missing on the sixth day was tranquillity. We must take care to ensure that when we seek to do service, charity, and social action, we carry a fragrance of tranquillity.

> Do you have the patience to wait
> till your mud settles and the water is clear?
> Can you remain unmoving
> till the right action arises by itself?

— TAO TE CHING

Sleeping on It

Jack was diagnosed with a painful ulcer. His doctors offered treatments that either gave him no relief or made him
uncomfortable. He decided, literally, to sleep on it. He had
a favorite cat that began, every night, to curl up on his
stomach. She would wiggle underneath the blankets as he
slept, and remain on his stomach all night long. She would
periodically get out, stretch, take some fresh air, and crawl
back in. Within two weeks Jack's ulcer was completely
healed.

Jesus' most poignant prayer—prayed when he knew he
was soon to die—was simply this: "Thy will be done."
This is not defeat or resignation, but astonishing faith that
there are spiritual forces that will bear him up, regardless of
the outcome. Often in our striving for a particular result,
we are not willing to be surprised by a healing we cannot
imagine. Paradoxically, it is often cowardice that makes us
hold on to our own small solutions; it takes infinitely more
courage to surrender.

*Think once again of a particular problem that concerns you.
Just as in the last exercise, imagine there are forces at work
that are already healing what needs to be healed; it only requires your surrender. Let it be. In the evening, turn it over to
the care of God, the angels, and all the Buddhas, all the spirits
of the earth and sky. When you awaken in the morning, look
at the problem again, and see what has grown there, quietly,
invisibly in the night.*

FROM ICE OUT

As late as yesterday ice preoccupied
the pond—dark, half-melted, waterlogged.
Then it sank in the night, one piece,
taking winter with it. And afterward
everything seems simple and good.

—JANE KENYON

NOBODY SPECIAL

Act as if everything depended on you;
trust as if everything
depended on God.
— SAINT IGNATIUS

Recently a wealthy New York couple withdrew their three-million-dollar donation to the Children's Zoo in Central Park because the city proposed a commemorative plaque that was smaller than the couple wanted. The modern world disdains selflessness. The important works are those that are signed, that get your photo in the paper, your name on the wall. Unless you are a Mother Teresa or a Dalai Lama, humility is decidedly out of fashion.

When I was ordained in the church, Henri Nouwen preached my ordination sermon. In the

Christian lineage, Jesus ordained Peter, who ordained a long line of priests, who eventually ordained Henri Nouwen, who put his hands on me. This is my lineage, an unbroken line of hands. My words and actions, if they bear fruit, come from the soil of that lineage.

When Henri preached at my ordination he told me to remember that the spiritual life was one of downward mobility. *Downward mobility*, he repeated several times, as if he worried I would forget. Indeed, I might have. I was fresh out of seminary, and had great spiritual feats to accomplish. I was prepared to dedicate myself to the service of others. Surely the honor and recognition to come would only be natural.

But Henri had another picture for me in his mind. Jesus insisted we do our work quietly, in secret. *Do not let your left hand know what your right hand is doing.* God's loving eye will see your good work in secret, and you will be rewarded in secret. Do not seek glory for yourself; the quiet reward is sweeter.

Henri's instruction to me was deeply authentic, from wisdom hard won. Henri had sold hundreds of thousands of books as a highly respected professor at Notre Dame, Yale, and Harvard. Still, he felt troubled and incomplete. He felt that his success and popularity camouflaged a deeper longing for quiet contemplation and service. In 1985 Henri left the comforts of the university to make his home as a chaplain in a small community of developmentally disabled adults.

In our many years as friends, there was never a question in my mind as to whom Henri was working for. Henri worked for Jesus. Even though he wrote often about himself in his books, it was never to show his strengths, but rather *to confess his weaknesses*. In weakness is the Lord's strength, said Saint Paul, and Henri was devoted to that theological premise. It made him human and accessible to those who worked quietly and tirelessly for their churches, for their communities, for those in need. He was not a superstar among the spiritual glitterati. But among those by whom service is performed invisibly and to great effect, he was revered and cherished as an indispensable companion. Whenever people learned I was a friend of Henri's, doors throughout the Christian world would be flung open with kindness and instant acceptance. *Oh, Henri,* they would say, and smile.

When Henri spoke of humility, he would often recount the story of Jesus who, after his baptism, spent forty days in the wilderness. After a long and arduous fast, Jesus was confronted by Satan, who tempted Jesus, inviting him to turn the stones lying on the dry ground into bread, thereby providing food for those who were hungry. Jesus refused, saying that we do not live by bread alone, but by the word of God. Then Satan suggested Jesus throw himself off the pinnacle of the temple, to demonstrate his celestial importance, as surely the angels themselves would bear him up. Again, Jesus refused. Finally, Satan offered Jesus unlimited power—full authority and dominion over all the kingdoms of the earth, if only Jesus would worship him. Jesus again refused, saying that one should worship only God.

According to Henri, Jesus' three temptations were these: To be useful. To be important. And to be powerful.

Useful, important, and powerful—are not these the attributes that still tempt every one of us who seek to do good in the world? Yet the saints and sages teach us to offer our kindness humbly, invisibly, quietly. Jesus did not seek worldly power or influence. He spent his time with unknown, disliked people. *Be faithful in small things,* he said, *and you will be faithful in great things.* He held up models: the Good Samaritan, who goes out of his way to help, completely anonymously, and seeks no reward; and the poor woman at the temple, who stealthily puts her two pennies into the collection box. As Mother Teresa reminded us, we do no great things, only small things with great love.

I was in bed one evening reading a political piece in *The New Yorker,* when I came upon Henri's name. It seemed that Hillary Clinton had been reading his writings on gratefulness and forgiveness. I called Henri and asked him about it. He told me that he had been invited to go to the White House to provide counsel during difficult times. While he sympathized with the Clintons' sorrows, and while a White House invitation seemed to be a recognition of the importance of spiritual matters, he nevertheless sent his apologies, and did not go. "I don't want to be the court chaplain," he told me. "I am here with Adam, my disabled friend. There are others who can go to the White House. Adam needs me." In that moment, I finally realized the full impact of his admonitions to me. Downward mobility.

Jesus was kind, loving, a peacemaker, humble, wise, a giving healer. The world saw this, took notice, and killed him for it. One of the things that died with Jesus was the illusion that the world will always reward good deeds. Sabbath is a time when we retreat from the illusion of our own indispensability. We are important in that we are part of something larger. We are part of the family of the earth, members of the body of Christ, part of the *dharma* and *sangha* of the Buddha. Our power comes not from ourselves, but from the enormousness of which we are a part.

True freedom comes when we become—as Zen teacher Suzuki Roshi said—"nobody special." We do our work not for glory and honor, but simply because we must, because we believe in the value of right action and good labor. In the end, we may or may not receive our reward from the world. More often, we receive our reward in secret. During a quiet walk, when we suddenly feel lighter; when we receive a kind word, and the heart is made warm and full; during a moment's reflection, when we feel a clarity of purpose, in these and a thousand other unexpected ways, we secretly receive our reward.

Sabbath time reminds us it is not by our hand but by earth and spirit and grace that all things are done. During Sabbath we take time, let things unfold without our influence, see how the earth feeds us, and remember that we are both creator and recipient of creation. We feel we must do everything ourselves—but what of the grace of God? What of the company of Jesus and the saints, what of the Buddha and the ministry of angels and bodhisattvas? We must help, but we are not in charge.

The word *humility*, like the word *human*, comes from *humus*, or earth. We are most human when we do no great things. We are not so important; we are simply dust and spirit—at best, loving midwives, participants in a process much larger than we. If we are quiet and listen and feel how things move, perhaps we will be wise enough to put our hands on what waits to be born, and bless it with kindness and care. But in the end, we are granted the tremendous blessing of knowing that we do very little at all by ourselves.

> When people praise me for something
> I vow with all being
> to return to my vegetable garden
> and give credit where credit is due.

— ROBERT AITKEN ROSHI

Humility

There was once a rabbi who, overcome with a sense of humility before God's magnificent creation, threw himself before the altar of the temple and cried, "I am nobody! I am nobody!"

The cantor, observing the rabbi from the rear of the synagogue, was moved by the rabbi's humility and devotion. He, too, joined the rabbi at the altar, crying, "I am nobody! I am nobody!"

Then the janitor, sweeping the floors in the hall, heard the cries of the two religious men and, similarly moved by their devotion, also joined them at the altar crying out, "I am nobody! I am nobody!"

At which point the cantor turned to the rabbi and, indicating the janitor, remarked, "Look who thinks he's nobody."

It is easier to feel a genuine sense of humility when we are alone. The instant others arrive we feel an impulse to compare, judge, puff up. It is useful to take some Sabbath time alone, for contemplation and reflection, for feeling the quieter truths of who we are, not in relation to work, prestige, accomplishments, or responsibilities, but to feel our place in relationship with the enormousness of creation. Helen and Trevor use the mornings to make love, and the afternoons to take quiet time alone. "We need them both," Trevor says. "After a long week we need to connect, but not just with each other. We also need to connect with ourselves."

The Desert Fathers counseled, "Go into your cell, and your cell will teach you everything." Set aside a period of time in nature or at home, at a church or temple, a library or anywhere you will not be disturbed. Sit, walk, meditate, pray, read, whatever pleases you. Pay attention.

BEING SABBATH

Let us remain as empty as possible
so that God can fill us up.
— MOTHER TERESA

As early as I can remember, I was both drawn to,
and pained by, the sorrows of others. I was pulled
toward their hurts, which, however they tried to hide
them, I saw as clearly as my own hands. For reasons I
did not then question, suffering people have always
come to me.

It didn't matter if it was Billy, who was over-
weight, or Melody, who always had hungry, lonely
eyes, who later killed herself in junior high. It didn't
matter if it was Barry whose brother always beat him
up, or the Nickersons who fought every day, their

angry screams punctuating summer evenings. Their son Toby was always a little awkward and unpredictable in a creepy sort of way, the kind of kid nobody ever wanted to play with, but everybody always made fun of. It didn't matter who they were, I befriended them all.

I saw the hurt in some of my parents' friends at the cocktail parties and card games and summer barbecues in the Long Island humidity, drinks sweating from the ice and moisture colliding over striped pastel plastic cocktail tumblers. I saw Mrs. P., my friend Jennifer's mom, try to get people to feel sorry for her, but no one seemed to want to hear about it, so I sat and listened, just to be nice, so she wouldn't feel so alone in her sad life.

Mr. Jackson, my supervisor when I worked as a garbage collector at Jones Beach in the summer, would tell me all about the dreams he had, the places he would go someday, even though I knew he heard the never-come-true in the stories he proudly conspired to share with me—a lowly sanitation worker—over ham sandwiches and warm Cokes.

Friends would fall in love; they would tell me first. When love went awry or broke into sharp, hurting pieces they cried at, with, to me first, in secret, always in secret.

It wasn't so much anything I did or said, as that I knew how to be invisible. To be empty, a zero, a place with nothing of my own to get in their way, a vacuum that sucked the stories out of them and into the safety of my company. I became the place they could be themselves, I was the ground where they planted their seeds of themselves and felt them grow, right there, they could feel it. Somehow my invisibility helped the quieter things in them become more visible.

As time evolved, this emptiness turned into a life, pulled me into relationship with people and suffering. I was drawn to where things hurt, and the hurt in them was drawn to me, some silent wordless chemical spiritual magnetism always at work, like the gravity between celestial bodies, people felled by their sadness, fear, loneliness found themselves in my orbit, circling, burning to enter my atmosphere. On line for a movie, with hundreds of people, the homeless man approaches me directly, only me, first and without hesitation. As a teenager I walked the streets of the Bowery in lower Manhattan; the street people would come to me and ask me to sit with them, smoke cigarettes, spill their disappointments into my lap.

When Tim Murphy, two years older than I in high school, went away on "retreat" with his youth group, he read a book, *A Separate Peace*, which awakened and devastated the tender, inner architecture of his adolescent heart. He came home and straight to my house, where he sat in my room, and wept in my arms. I remember thinking even then, *This is not about me*.

Others have also been Sabbath for me. When I was eighteen I was already a sophomore in college, having skipped a grade in elementary school. Over the years I had at times used my intellect to mask my feelings. After completing my freshman year with a 4.0 average, I thought I would transfer from the University of Rochester to Harvard, for more stimulation, prestige, and intellectual opportunity. I went to see the school counseling service to get permission to transfer, and to negotiate about the particulars.

The counselor was a very wise man. He saw instantly that behind the mental bravado there was tenderness and pain, and that my heart was deeply confused. He listened patiently to my plans and strategies, and when I finished he said nothing about my ambitions or my schemes. After a period of silence, he simply said, "You seem sad." I was completely taken by surprise. I felt frightened and dizzy. Suddenly I began to weep, deep, racking sobs. I wept for the better part of an hour. I wept for all the loneliness in my life, for the pains of my childhood, for unnameable wounds and achings in my soul. He guided me to the carpet and let me lie on the floor, where he held my hand as I wept. His kind, quiet presence changed my life. A single moment, a touch, a Sabbath moment's undivided attention was all that was required.

I became a student of this man, and through his suggestion I volunteered as a phone counselor at the suicide hotline.

Once a woman called to describe her despair, and how she was going to end her life. She would call and ask for me; every week we talked for hours. I wanted to be an English teacher, but here I was, at midnight, a vessel for the sorrow of an invisible woman. Later she would come to visit me, strictly prohibited by all the rules; still, she had to come, to say in person I had saved her life. I never did or said anything particularly wise or dramatic. But somehow our conversations had become Sabbaths for her.

Years later, I am a family therapist in the inner city, working with poor and neglected children. I go up the stairs of a government housing project—one of the first built many hopeful years ago—now old, many of the windows broken out, cool in the dark corridors and gray winter light.

Inside, she sits at the kitchen table. So many meetings at so many kitchen tables. This is where truths are shared, hearts unburdened. Where the food is. She speaks of her deep love and concern. Her ten-year-old son is under the care of the white judge and the white probation officer and now I, the white counselor, have come to rescue this boy from who-knows-what destiny. We sit without words. I could sit quietly in her kitchen all day by that stove. I am fed by the warmth, the empty quiet, the Sabbath. I wish I were her son, so deeply does she care for him. I am nourished by the Sabbath of our silence in her kitchen.

What is the right thing? Neither of us has words that would give birth to anything we could call a happy ending. The whole myth of organized helpfulness feels like a barren setup, a foiled relationship, even when we all try so hard, and mean so well. There are larger forces at work. It dawns on me why prayer is the only reasonable practice. Poor people always ask me to pray with them, and it feels like the one time something real happens, because it is not about our skill or our will, but rather our humility and helplessness laid bare.

Today, twenty-five years later, they still call me. A lover is murdered. A child dies in her sleep. I sit quietly and say, *Yes, yes,* quietly, again, *Oh, yes.* No struggle, no promised land, no happy ending, no good reason. Only the faint, inevitable sound of forms crumbling, creation returning to quiet, a surrender to emptiness, and hands holding hands. This is not about me, not about them. It is life making itself known in the quiet tearing of flesh, the silent Sabbath of things yet unknown taking birth.

Others share with me how they are Sabbath for one another. Margaret is a patient coordinator at a large urban hospice center. "After years of running from patients to meetings and writing reports and calling volunteers I have finally learned that my real job, when dealing with dying patients, is to be calm, the eye of the storm." When she can feel the time for paperwork, prescriptions, treatment plans, and casework has ended, Margaret allows herself to sit with those in need of her company, and gradually become still, like deep water. In these moments Margaret becomes the Sabbath for her patients. Into her emptiness they pour their souls. The sick and dying plant their fear and sadness in the ground of her quiet, where together, in time that cannot be measured by any clock, they enter into Sabbath time. And in that time there grows a peace that passes understanding.

At our best, we become Sabbath for one another. We are the emptiness, the day of rest. We become space, that our loved ones, the lost and sorrowful, may find rest in us. *Whenever two or more are gathered, there am I in the midst of you.* Not fixing, not harming, not acting. Quietly empty, we become Sabbath, where the sorrows of the world are safely poured and gently dissolve into the unfathomable immensity of rest, and silence.

YEATS:

We can make our minds so like still water that beings gather about us, that they may see their own images, and so live for a moment with a clearer, perhaps even a fiercer life, life because of our quiet.

Thinning

I've been noticing what has to be simplified is the abundance in my life—all the opportunity. The metaphor for this is my garden. We have an abundance of growing vegetables—we planted turnips, carrots, daikon radishes, lettuce, herbs, tomatillos, eggplant—they started growing riotously—I couldn't believe how you could plant seeds and then all this stuff would just come up with abandon. I knew I needed to thin those turnips and carrots—but I just couldn't bring myself to do it. I thought maybe they'll grow anyway. So I never did thin or prune those turnips and carrots. They also never did grow. Not one turnip did I get—although there were tons of greens. So I've been reflecting on why I don't want to thin the things in my life that I need to—I just keep holding on for dear life, but those turnips are telling me what will happen if I don't create space for growth, space for life, space for spirit.

Thinning is, as Frances says, making space for life. We plant so many seeds, and they seem so small, so benign, they take up hardly any space at all. But everything, as it grows, needs space. Children, a home, a career, a project, a hobby, a spiritual practice, everything needs space, and everything needs time. And as each grows, each one takes from the other, until nothing grows beneath the surface, it is all foliage and greenery aboveground, and no nutrition beneath. Sooner or later, it all withers from lack of nourishment.

What can you let go of? One thing, beginning with the smallest thing. A book unread—can it be given to the library? An old postcard on the refrigerator, no longer current? An old appliance, never used? Old clothing, never worn, to the poor? What of projects that feel like responsibilities but bring joy to no one? Pick one thing this week, another the next, and discard something that has become unnecessary. Feel any release as you let it go.

BEGINNER'S MIND

An old Hasidic rabbi crosses the village square every morning on his way to the temple to pray. One morning, a large Cossack soldier, who happened to be in a vile mood, accosted him, saying, "Hey, Rebby, where are you going?"

And the rabbi said, "I don't know."

This infuriated the Cossack. "What do you mean, you don't know? Every morning for twenty-five years you have crossed the village square and gone to the temple to pray. Don't fool with me. Who are you, telling me you don't know?"

He grabbed the old rabbi by the coat and dragged him off to jail. Just as he was about to push him into the cell, the rabbi turned to him, saying: "You see, I didn't know."

— TRADITIONAL TALE

When we plant a garden, we begin with a clear idea of what we will plant, how many and how deep the rows, and how we will care for what we have planted. Yet we cannot know whether there will be drought or flood, heat or cold, which seeds will do well, what bugs or diseases will emerge this season, or how the harvest will be. We can work hard to anticipate these things, but some of our efforts will be fruitful, and some will not. This is the nature of all life, moved by silent forces larger than we can ever comprehend.

Thomas Merton begins this oft-repeated prayer with a confession: *My dear God, I have no idea where I am going. I do not see the road ahead of me. I cannot know for certain where it will end.* In a similar way Suzuki Roshi exalts the virtue of what he calls "beginner's mind," a condition of being able to embrace and accept a certain level of inevitable unknowing. It is, he says, a fertile practice, because often it is when we do not know the outcome that all things become possible.

Alisa told me that her father had prostate cancer. For twenty years he had faithfully gone to his doctor to get his annual prostate screening. He took his doctor's advice at every turn, exercised, and ate a very healthy diet. He was both proud and confident, and often boasted about his robust health. But when he found he was sick with cancer, he felt sad and defeated, cheated somehow. He knew what to do to prevent cancer, and he did it. He was certain his careful preparations had made him immune.

Just because we are working hard does not mean we are making anything happen. Our best-laid plans and goals and performance evaluations do not guarantee that what we desire will actually come about. They may make us feel more confident or in control, but that is as often as not an illusion that may very well be shattered by the unpredictable unfolding of destiny. If we keep working, we feel we are actually controlling events. Knowledge is power, they say, and when we do not know, we feel powerless and afraid.

There is an old Taoist story about a wise man on the northern frontier of China. One day, for no apparent reason, a young man's horse ran away and was taken by nomads across the border. Everyone tried to offer consolation for the man's ill fortune, but his father, a wise man, said, "What makes you so sure this is not a blessing?"

Months later, his horse returned, bringing with her a magnificent stallion. This time everyone was full of congratulations for the son's good fortune. But now his father said, "What makes you so sure this isn't a disaster?" Their household was made richer by this fine horse, which the son loved to ride. But one day he fell off the horse and broke his hip. Once again, everyone offered their consolation for his bad luck, but his father said, "What makes you so sure this is not a blessing?"

A year later the nomads mounted an invasion across the border, and every able-bodied man was required to take up his bow and go into battle. The Chinese frontiersmen lost nine of every ten men. Only because the son was lame did father and son survive to take care of each other. Truly, the story reminds us, blessing turns to disaster, and disaster to blessing: The changes have no end, nor can the mystery be fathomed.

I met my dear friends Jim and Caroline when I first moved to Santa Fe. They had recently moved from the Midwest, where Jim had worked for many years for the John Deere Tractor Company. They had both worked hard, raised their children, saved their money, and built a home in Santa Fe. They had great plans for fully enjoying their many years ahead, and their home was designed specifically so their children could come often and visit.

Two years after their retirement, Jim died suddenly of pancreatic cancer. His family was devastated. Caroline always believed she would live out her life with her best friend and beloved husband. For many years she grieved his tragic and unexpected death, struggling to create a life without his loving companionship.

Recently, Caroline wrote me a letter.

I'm moving toward an acceptance of "not knowing." I hope I am developing humility, which has come about not through logical deduction but through the pain of loss. Simply not trying to analyze and interpret every dream or event . . . Sometimes I find that the surprising, the unlooked-for, or even the unwanted has rewards that are not immediately apparent.

Rewards that are not immediately apparent. When we are used to instant gratification, quicker news, microwaved food, faster computers, we are reluctant to let things go unknown or unfinished for long periods of time. We want to know immediately what is going to happen next. We want instant weather, stock market quotes, public opinion polls, and interest rates. But in the end, the most important things show themselves slowly, and in their own time. How will our children grow? Will we be happy? How will we die? Will we be at peace?

In the quiet, the truth emerges: I do not know where I am going. I am riding a wave I cannot see. *The wind blows where it will, and we hear the sound of it, but we cannot tell from whence it comes or whither it goes. Such is the way of the spirit.* A woman awakes to find her nine-year-old daughter dead, an aneurysm in the night. Another woman finds a lump in her breast. A third woman falls unexpectedly in love. We do not know how it will go. Only inertia and faith keep us upright— and still we worry, and often.

Sabbath invites endless beginnings. We begin anew each week, renewing our preconceptions, indeed our very life, a beginner again and again. Sometimes, when we feel trapped by a problem, we must surrender to not knowing the solution. Sometimes it is only when we let the problem alone, when we back off in unknowing, that it has the space to solve itself.

Edward Gibbon conceived his history of the rise and fall of the Roman Empire while listening to a choir of monks at vespers. Nobel physicist Steven Weinberg was nagged by the problem of how nuclear reactions produce the heat of the sun—until it came to him one day unbidden as he was driving around Boston in his red Camaro. Allegedly, Archimedes discovered the law of specific gravity while taking a bath. Sometimes our greatest wisdom comes when we are not striving to discover anything at all.

Hume Cronyn, the actor, worked with Alfred Hitchcock, a famously exacting director. "One time," Cronyn recounts, "we were working on a problem with a scene. There were a lot of things to consider—lighting, staging, pacing, and the like. We were up very late struggling to find the right way to do it. Finally, when we seemed close to the solution, Hitchcock came in and started telling jokes, silly, junior high–type stuff, and got us all lost again. Later, I asked him why, when we were so close to solving the problem, did he choose that moment to get us off track by joking around? He paused, and then said something I'll never forget. He said, 'You were pushing. It never comes from pushing.' "

Not long ago I was speaking with Hans-Peter Durr, who for twenty years collaborated with Nobel Prize winner Werner Heisenberg, discoverer of the famous Uncertainty Principle in quantum physics. Himself a noted quantum physicist, Hans-Peter told me that he often had long, impassioned discussions with Heisenberg when they were working together on a particular problem. "We would be talking excitedly about the problem from every angle, and then suddenly Heisenberg would say, 'Wait, I think we have touched something very important here. Let's not talk about it any more. Let's wait for two weeks, and let it solve itself.' Then, when we got together two weeks later, it would invariably be solved. We would begin talking, and we both knew we had the answer."

Sabbath honors this quality of not knowing, an open receptivity of mind essential for allowing things to speak to us from where they are. If we take a day and rest, we cultivate Sabbath Mind. We let go of knowing what will happen next, and find the courage to wait for the teaching that has not yet emerged. The presumption of the Sabbath is that *it is good*, and that the wisdom, courage, and clarity we need are already embedded in creation. The solution is already alive in the problem. Our work is not always to push and strive and struggle. Sometimes we have only to be still, says the Psalmist, and we will know.

Cleansing

Rachel is a busy professional woman in corporate life. She used to strive for ever-increasing efficiency so that she could get more done. "I even cut my hair very short so that I could save time shampooing and drying my hair in the morning. I figured I could get to work that much earlier."

Now, after several bouts with arthritis that leave her bending with pain, she moves more slowly, thoughtfully, more mindful of what can be done without haste. She takes a Sabbath bath three evenings a week. For anywhere from thirty minutes to an hour and a half, she draws a warm bath, lights candles, adds fragrance. She installed a skylight above her bath so she can watch the movements of the trees, planted in the 1930's, as they grow old together. She lets her husband and children know she is not to be disturbed, and they honor her bath time. She prays, she says, quietly, sometimes weeping, sometimes in peaceful meditation. It is a deep cleansing, deeper than mere skin or body, but a soul cleansing. She has let her hair grow long.

Sabbath is traditionally preceded by ritual bathing, a cleansing of the old, a preparation to receive the new. This allows a visceral sense of beginner's body as well as beginner's mind. Hands are washed before the meal, bodies are bathed before making love. Ritual cleansing, more than the soap and water, opens us to receive anew. Set aside some time for bathing, long and easy, with fragrances, candles, music. Pay attention to your body, wash yourself gently and with care for every inch of skin. Bathe yourself as a mother bathes her beloved child.

CAMAS LILIES

Consider the lilies of the field,
the blue banks of camas opening
into acres of sky along the road.
Would the longing to lie down
and be washed by that beauty
abate if you knew their usefulness,
how the natives ground their bulbs
for flour, how the settlers' hogs
uprooted them, grunting in gleeful
oblivion as the flowers fell?

And you—what of your rushed and
useful life? Imagine setting it all down—
papers, plans, appointments, everything—
leaving only a note: "Gone to the fields
to be lovely. Be back when I'm through
with blooming."

Even now, unneeded and uneaten, the
camas lilies gaze out above the grass
from their tender blue eyes.
Even in sleep your life will shine.
Make no mistake.
Of course
your work will always matter.
Yet Solomon in all his glory
was not arrayed like one of these.

— LYNN UNGAR

CONSECRATION

MINDFULNESS AND
HOLINESS

Remember the Sabbath day, to keep it holy.

— EXODUS 20:8

Ｎew Mexico struggles with one of the highest rates of drunk driving fatalities in the nation. The sides of many roads are punctuated with crosses, marking the places where children, mothers, fathers, whole families were killed. Each cross is adorned with gifts, pictures, and handwritten notes wrapped in plastic to keep off the rain. Family and friends regularly visit these spots, bring fresh flowers, pray, and remember. Each patch of ground is made sacred by the enormity of what happened there, and the holiness is sustained by the tears and love poured into the soil in which the cross is planted.

In this spot the veil was torn, and one of our own was catapulted through the membrane of life and death. We mark those places where lives were taken; we feel them set apart, and bring our gifts and prayers and remembrances. Just as a church stands where Jesus prayed, or a mosque where Mohammed received a vision, we know this ground is holy. It is consecrated partly because of what happened there, and partly because it is a magnet for our devotion. It is the same if you go to St. Patrick's or Notre Dame, to Bodh Gaya or the smallest village chapel. Stop and listen: You can still hear all the prayers ever prayed there; they roam the air, they live in the wind, they carry our hearts to heaven.

Sabbath time can be like this, a sanctuary in time when we consecrate our loved ones, our yearnings for peace, our prayers for strength and well-being for our children. We consecrate them, we *en-holy* them, with our mindfulness, gratefulness, and care. If we are too busy to see them, hold them, or play with them, they escape our blessing, and we are bereft of theirs. Our wealth arises from our capacity to bless and be blessed. We are not blessed because we are wealthy; we are wealthy because we take time to bless.

Remember the Sabbath, and keep it holy. Sabbath time is set apart for remembering the holiness of life. If we speed up and saturate ourselves with accomplishment and worry, we may defile what is sacred with our mindlessness. Time is the key. Time, and attention. If we grab a sandwich as we run out the door, this is eating. If we take a small crust of bread and a sip of wine, in a mindful gathering of other beings, this is a sacrament. It is neither the food nor the eating but the time and the mindfulness that reveal what is holy.

Justine's mother died after a long illness, and was cremated. Her mother loved the sea, and wanted her ashes to be scattered by the water. Justine chose a particular day, rose early, and, beginning with prayer and meditation, consecrated the day as a holy vessel in which her mother's ashes could be carried home.

On the way over the mountains to the ocean, Justine began to imagine how sad she would feel when she scattered her mother's ashes. She wondered if she would cry, or if she would feel lonely and bereft as she let her mother go. All along the way she preoccupied her mind with thoughts of how tender an event it would be. But when she arrived at the beach she realized she had created a movie in her mind of the perfect good-bye, and that the greatest gift for them both would be for her to simply be attentive and aware. She decided she would just let it be as it was. Let it happen as it would.

She walked to the water, and stood in quiet contemplation, allowing the fullness of time to wash over her. Then she lifted the urn and opened it, took a handful of her mother's ashes, and began to pray. As she prayed there for her mother's peace, for her life and death, for her eternal rest, a wind came up of a sudden and swept the ashes from her hand, lifting them and scattering them all over the beach. The ashes in the urn swirled out, too, her mother's ashes playing in the wind like a dance of celebration. "I was engulfed in a swirl of mother," she said.

Now, years later, Justine sometimes goes back to that beach, often taking along Hillary, her very special four-year-old friend. Hillary knows the story about Justine's mother, and how her ashes were scattered by the sea. Today, when Hillary reaches the ocean, she bends down and picks up a pinch of sand. "Is this your mother?" she asks. "Yes," Justine replies, and smiles. Hillary draws the sand to her lips, kisses it, and lets it go.

Consecration.

Confession

Jules and Olivia are in their fifties, and even though their children are grown, they love to celebrate Shabbos. Every Friday night, before the Sabbath meal, they draw a warm bath and, together, take off their clothes and bathe. This is their ritual cleansing, part of their marriage covenant, preparation to receive the Sabbath bride. But more than this, it is also a time for intimacies, and confession.

Each unclothed and open to receive the other, they each put a hand to the other's heart, and ask if there is anything they need to say, any confession, something lingering in the heart that, left unsaid, would hinder a full and joyful Sabbath. On some nights, there is little to say. On other nights, words must be spoken aloud that have lived in secret. Who can imagine what lovers must share, when seeking a pure heart and an honest Sabbath? For thirty years, such honesty comes to this: two beings, warm and close, bathed in love.

Confession—it is said—is good for the soul. Before Mass, Catholics practice confession, a ritual cleansing before receiving the gift of communion. Not to receive punishment or even absolution, but rather to speak what must be brought out from darkness, if we are to receive the light.

Before Sabbath time, choose a quiet place. Come to rest. Allow the heart and mind to speak of things that need to be spoken aloud, if only to the candle on the altar. Say aloud those things for which you feel a need for forgiveness, ways in which you were not clear, honest, or kind. If you feel comfortable, you can share this with another—a priest, minister, or rabbi, a therapist, a friend, a stranger. Notice how much of your grasping during the week is to make these things go away. Notice how they dissolve so much more easily when they are simply spoken aloud.

THE WAY OF ENOUGH

I make myself rich by making my wants few.
— THOREAU

When the people of Israel wandered in exile, hungry in the wilderness, they cried out to God for food. God fed them with manna from heaven, bread that "was like coriander seed, white, and the taste of it was like wafers made with honey." Aside from its sweetness, the other definitive quality of manna was that it would not keep overnight. God, through Moses, told them to "gather of it, each one of you, as much as you can eat." However, no one was to leave any of it till morning. If anyone took more than they needed and kept it overnight, by morning it would breed worms and become foul. This was to remind them that each day, whatever was given would be enough.

Similarly, after the Buddha died, his followers gathered to consider the precepts by which they would live. One of the first monastic principles concerned food: Monks could not keep food overnight. Each morning they would have to beg for their daily bread. Making the rounds of the village with their begging bowl, they would learn that whatever was given would be enough.

Lynn Twist is a friend who has dedicated her life to eliminating world hunger. She has traveled around the world, working on behalf of starving children. She tells me that our search for "abundance"—so common in contemporary spiritual circles—is actually fed by a lingering belief in scarcity. If we are afraid there is not enough for us, we will grab for abundance—which is actually *more* than we need. Thus, even in abundance, there is great fear.

Adrian separated from and divorced her husband of ten years. Along with her two small children, she moved into a tiny home and began to worry about the future, how she would provide for her family. "I was so scared," she said. "I went out and, with some of my savings, bought a half a cow, had it butchered, and froze it in a freezer in our garage. I had never been on my own, and was terrified we would not have enough to eat. I thought having an abundance of food would make me feel safe. But it wasn't really abundance; all that food just reminded me how scared I was."

Lynn makes a crucial distinction between *abundance*—a fearful response to scarcity—and *sufficiency*—which invokes an experience of satisfaction and well-being. Sufficiency is that moment when we have enough. What is enough? After a meal, our craving for food dissolves. After we have arrived at our destination, we no longer need the map that brought us there. After a drink from a cool fountain, we are no longer desperate to find water. The instant we have enough, dissatisfaction and desire melt away.

In the Hebrew tradition, petitionary prayer is discouraged

during Sabbath time. We focus our heart not on what we need, but rather on what we have. When we are attentive and awake, a single breath can fill us to overflowing. The touch of a loved one, a particular angle of sunlight can bring delight to our hearts. The simple gesture of someone's hand resting in our own, a taste of honey, or a strain of melody can give birth to quiet satisfaction, a sense of enough.

A woman at a retreat shared how she had devoted her whole life to spiritual seeking. She had traveled to sacred sites, attended countless retreats and workshops, sought teachers and guides. It had, she confessed, been a time of much striving; it had been fruitful in some ways, yet she felt tired, weary. She was getting older. She wondered how much stamina she had left to continue her search.

"You have been a seeker for so long," I said. "Why not become a finder? At this stage in your life, what if you imagined you were ready to let go of seeking, and begin finding?" She remained silent for a time, a look of deep confusion on her face, her head slightly tilted, as if she were trying to hear a sound far away. Then, suddenly, a laugh exploded from deep in her belly. A finder! What a delight! How could she have never imagined it before? She had always been so focused on the search, she had never taken time to rejoice in the blessing, the gift of finding.

When we are trapped in seeking, nothing is enough. Everything we have mocks us; we see only what is missing, and all that is already here seems pale and unsatisfying. In Sabbath time we bless what there is for being. The time for seeking is over; the time for finding has begun.

Many of the world's religions were born in deserts, places with very little food or water. At rest, we may be surprised how, even in the driest places, we are quickly filled to sufficiency by the multitude of gratuitous offerings that arise in a single Sabbath afternoon.

A Place at the Table

Tracy looked out her window one Sunday morning and saw a disheveled man sleeping on the park bench across the street. "I made up a bag lunch just like the one I would give my son for school: sandwich, apple, a couple of cookies, a can of soda." (The latter was not standard issue, she assured me.) "I took it over to the man when he woke up. What he did next I will never forget. He sat up straight on the bench and carefully spread out one of the paper napkins, lining it up square on the seat. Then he slowly unpacked the bag and laid out each item on the napkin. He could not have been more ceremonial if he had been dining in a fine restaurant. When I think of consecration, that is the image that comes to me."

When we gather for a Sabbath meal, we partake of the spiritual companionship of all who have loved us, all we love, all who have gone before and will come after. Everyone we have touched, those who have taught or held or nourished us all come to the table. It is good to be mindful of our ancestors, our loved ones, our extended family who could not join us in body for this blessed meal. So when you eat, set a place, complete with plate, glass, and silverware, an empty place to hold the awareness of all who join you there in spirit. During Passover, Jews set this place specifically for Elijah, awaiting his promised return. But for any sacred meal, it is good to leave a place of invitation, mindful of all those with whom we are, now and forever, consecrated family.

OWNERSHIP

Where your treasure is,
there will your heart be also.

— MATTHEW 6:21

Whatever we place at the center of our lives will
get the bulk of our care and attention. This is not
esoteric teaching, but simple physics. If we love our
children more than anything, they will get the best of
our attention. If we love success, our career will get
the majority of our time. If we love money, we will
spend the greater portion of our care and worry on the
accumulation of wealth.

Recognizing this law, most spiritual traditions
counsel us to be mindful of what we possess. In Christianity there is a precept called *the vow of poverty*. This

vow is almost universally misinterpreted as declaring that all material possessions are bad or evil. Owning things or having wealth will, the popular thinking goes, inevitably taint our soul, and poison our spiritual purity.

Yet both King David and King Solomon were fabulously rich, and it didn't seem to bother God at all. The problem is not material possessions in themselves as much as the way we live our lives once we have them. The more possessions and riches we have, the more time we must provide for their care, maintenance, inventory, insurance, and protection—and the less time we will have for prayer, for God and neighbor, for friendship, kindness, peace, and rest. Riches may enable us to buy things that may bring happiness for a short while—until we realize we are spending all our time taking care of all our things, and hardly any time actually enjoying our children, lovers, friends, or nature. Things are not the problem; the time it takes to buy things, have things, and take care of things is the problem. This is the fundamental wisdom of the vow of poverty.

Everything we invite into our lives requires a certain measure of time and attention—usually more than we think when we acquire it. So our days, especially our time "off," our evenings and weekends, end up being dedicated to keeping all our possessions in working order. The invitation to poverty is not an invitation to suffer deprivation, but rather to consider whether the things we have acquired are really serving us— or are we serving them?

Mulla Nasrudin was eating a poor man's diet of chickpeas and bread. His neighbor, who also claimed to be a wise man, was living in a grand house and dining upon sumptuous meals provided by the emperor himself.

His neighbor told Nasrudin, "If only you would learn to flatter the emperor and be subservient as I do, you would not have to live on chickpeas and bread."

Nasrudin replied, "And if only you would learn to live on chickpeas and bread, as I do, you would not have to flatter and live subservient to the emperor."

The Hebrew practice of Sabbath included honoring the Sabbath year, when people refrained from planting, sowing seed, or harvesting crops. During this fallow time—an entire year of rest—the community relied upon whatever grew in the fields of its own. This served as a dramatic reminder that it was not their work alone, but rather God and the earth who fed them. Further, every seventh Sabbath year—every forty-ninth year, the Year of Jubilee—all lands that were sold or confiscated were returned to their original owners, all debts canceled, and all prisoners set free. The Sabbath teaching was clear: Nothing really belongs to us. It is all—lands, wealth, loved ones, life itself—on loan from God.

Whatever we hold as our own, however briefly, we consecrate with our very life. This alone should give us pause before we invite anything or anyone new into our already crowded and hurried lives. During Sabbath we consecrate our lives, our friends and family, our community, and the earth itself with our prayers, our mindfulness, even our delight. How much can we hold, how much can we take in, and still have room to bestow our full-hearted blessing?

HOW TO OWN LAND

Find a spot and sit there
until the grass begins
to nose between your thighs.

Climb to the top
of a pine and drink
the wind's green breath.

Track the stream through alder and scrub,
trade speech
for that cold sweet babble.

Gather sticks and spin them into fire.
Watch the smoke spiral into darkness.
Dream that the animals find you.

They weave your hair into warm cloth,
string your teeth on necklaces,
wrap your skin soft around their feet.

Wake to the silence
of your own scattered bones.
Watch them whiten in the sun.

When they have fallen to powder
and blown away,
the land will be yours.

— MORGAN FARLEY

Giveaway

Many native cultures measure wealth not by what one possesses, but by what one feels able to give away. They celebrate *potlatch*, or the great giveaway, when gifts are freely given to others in the community. These are not leftovers or castoffs, as we give to the Salvation Army Thrift Store; nor are they hastily purchased trinkets. Rather, they give away the best of what they own, their finest. If we can afford to give away our best—if we can give away what we love the most—then we must be very wealthy, indeed.

The Buddha said that if we truly understood the power of giving, we would never let even a single meal pass without sharing it with someone. Go through your home, and look at what you have accumulated, especially the beautiful, inspiring, or nourishing things. If you decided to make a gift of something to someone, how would you decide what to give? And who should receive it? Can you imagine giving it away, not to gain favor or reciprocity, but completely gratuitously? Pick something, pick someone to receive it, and give it away. This is the beginning of true wealth.

BREAKING THE TRANCE

We are most deeply asleep at the switch
when we fancy we control
any switches at all. We sleep
to time's hurdy-gurdy;
we wake, if we ever wake,
to the silence of God.
— ANNIE DILLARD

When we go to a movie, the lights go dark and we enter the world on the screen. We are seduced by the illusion on the film. Still images of actors in front of a camera in a Hollywood studio are flashed on the screen one after another in rapid succession, so that it fools our eyes; our mind eliminates the blank spaces between frames, and makes it look like seamless movement. Slowly, we surrender even our emotions to the illusion and enter into the world of the "characters" on the screen, coming to know them, care for them, even worry about them. Our body responds, our heart beats faster, perhaps we laugh or weep, as if we were actually present and involved in that world.

We become enraptured with the place in which they live. Maybe they are to be lovers, we do not know yet; she is beautiful but she may not want him—will she kiss him or betray him? Yet look, there is a slight movement of her head, a tilt in his direction, barely perceptible, but maybe, yet, suddenly yes she will. . . .

Bam! Suddenly, the film breaks, the lights come on. It is very disorienting at first; we do not know where we are, or what is happening. Slowly we remember, we are in a theater; we remember we came here in a car, we just had dinner, that our life here is not the life on the screen at all. The images, those people were an illusion. Slowly, our life comes pouring back into ourselves.

We were seduced into a trance, a pleasant illusion, one to which we willingly submit ourselves whenever we enter a movie theater, television program, or good novel. But when the trance is broken, it takes a while to let go of the "truth" of the life into which we had completely surrendered.

In the same way we can, over time, become enthralled in the trance of our work. It is all-important, it must be done right away, it won't get done without me, I cannot stop or it will all fall apart, it is all up to me, terrible things will happen if I do not get this done. I have to keep working because I have things to buy and there are bills to pay for those things and I have to buy faster computers and more expensive telephones to help me get more done so I can keep up and make money to pay the bills for the things I need to buy to help me get these things done . . .

Once we are in this trance, there never seems to be a good enough reason to stop. The wisdom of Sabbath time is that at a prescribed moment, it is time to stop. We cannot wait until we are finished, because we are never finished. We cannot wait until we have everything we need, because the mind is seduced by endlessly multiplying desires. We cannot wait until things slow down, because the world is moving faster and faster, and we cannot be left behind. There are always a million good reasons to keep on going, and never a good enough reason to stop.

In Chinese medicine, the first step in treatment is to break the old pattern. Only when the unhealthy pattern is interrupted can healing be possible. Jack is a television producer who works eighteen-hour days. It is not unusual for him to get to the office to find up to one hundred messages on his answering machine. "At times," he tells me, "I am so tightly wound, it seems I never come completely unwound." He feels both fascinated and repulsed by seductions of money and success; but lately he has begun to notice how they crowd out any possibility of kindness or reflection. "Only when I am relaxed—and that happens much less than I would like—does compassion flow more easily from me, to myself and others. Then, I can view people not in terms of what they can do for me, and my local community becomes a garden of people and places. I develop an interest in people I have never seen before. Maybe I strike up a conversation with the woman at the dry cleaner's. I stop seeing people solely for their function, and start seeing their value." Speaking of the Sabbath, which he has occasionally observed in his home, he says, "When you are quiet, resting, singing, and eating Shabbos candy, it is harder to imagine cutting someone off on the way to a sale at Barney's."

One of the astonishing attributes of Sabbath time is its unflinching uselessness. Nothing will get done, not a single item will be checked off any list. Nothing of significance will be accomplished, no goal realized. It is thoroughly without measurable value. Many of us are reluctant to slow our pace because we feel a driving need to be useful. Nancy, a hard-working, well-respected executive, feels it is difficult for her to take Sabbath time because "I am driven by the need to be useful; I have a sense of constantly having to justify my existence. It keeps me tied to the wheel. I envy people who feel they can just lounge around, much more than I envy rich people."

During the week our work, our contributions to the well-being of our family and community are essential and necessary. But Sabbath time offers the gift of deep balance; in Sabbath time, we are valued not for what we have done or accomplished, but simply because we have received the gentle blessing of being miraculously alive. Just as the unborn child in the womb of its mother silently receives an endless supply of nourishment, warmth, and protection, so, during Sabbath time, does the sweet womb of sacred rest enfold us, nourish us, heal and restore us.

These are the useless things that grow in time: To walk without purpose, to no place in particular, where we are astonished by the textured bark of an oak. To notice the color red showing itself for the first time in the maple in fall. To see animals in the shapes of clouds, to walk in clover. To fall into an unexpected conversation with a stranger, and find something delicious and unbidden take shape. To taste the orange we eat, the juice on the chin, the pulp between teeth. To take a deep sigh, an exhale, followed by a listening silence. To allow a recollection of a moment with a loved one, a feeling of how our life has evolved. To give thanks for a single step upon the earth. To give thanks for any blessing, previously unnoticed; the gentle brush of a hand on a lover's body, the sweet surrender of sleep in the afternoon.

At one retreat there was a woman, a potter. She had been having difficulty with her pots. She would center her clay, and then kept bringing it out, out, to its edge, and then, pushed to its limit, it would collapse. Over and over she would center it again, raise it, bring it out to its farthest edge, and it would collapse. Eventually she would tire of this challenge, of pushing the clay to its edge, and reluctantly surrender to the fact that she needed to keep the clay closer to the center.

As she spoke of it, in this quiet room filled with Sabbath

pilgrims, she recognized something she had missed. She realized that she was not the potter; *she was the clay*. She had been brought again and again to her edge, only to collapse.

The invitation was clear, to live her life close to her center. Properly centered, the clay would hold.

A SABBATH DAY

This sketch offers a few suggestions to help you begin to shape a Sabbath day. Like the practices at the end of each chapter, the prayers, rituals, and other activities are merely samples. As you become more comfortable with Sabbath time, you will undoubtedly discover personal rituals that enable you to more fully enjoy this time of sacred rest.

EVENING

Sabbath time can begin in the evening, emerging as soft, inner light at the darkening of day. Or Sabbath can begin at morning, a fresh beginning taking birth with the promise of the new day. Christian and Jewish traditions draw heavily on both evening and morning time. The Jewish Sabbath begins as the sun sets, while many Catholic churches now begin Sunday Sabbath with a Mass on Saturday evening. While Christians traditionally begin Sunday with some form of church worship, prayer, or family gathering, Jews also use

Sabbath morning as an opportunity to gather at the synagogue for prayer and worship.

If Sabbath begins at evening, reading some form of scripture—often psalms—gently alters the quality of our attention. You may want to include poetry or other spiritual reflection of your own choosing. Lorraine says that when she reads scripture on Sabbath evening, she can actually feel the *neshemah yeterah*, the additional soul we are said to be given during Sabbath, the better to delight and apprehend the blessings of the day. She feels the soul fill her, she says, and the tension leaves her body.

In the Jewish tradition, after ritual bathing, the woman of the household lights the two Sabbath candles, offering a blessing. When you light your candles, offer any blessing that reflects the thoughts of your heart.

> May our hearts be lifted, our spirits refreshed, as we light the Sabbath candles. May the light fill our home with kindness and peace. Blessed is the loving spirit by whose power we consecrate the lighting of these candles.

Like the sounding of a bell that calls the monks to meditation, as the lighting of the candles begins the Mass, as the lighting of the candles begins Sabbath time, so does the lighting of these candles call our souls to rest and delight.

RIANE EISLER:

> I was born into a Viennese Jewish family, and when the Nazis took over we fled to Cuba. There my parents kept up Jewish traditions. Praying with my family gave me some of my most precious childhood memories. My mother baked bread for the Shabbat, and every Shabbat she lit the holiday candles. Have you ever seen a woman in the Jewish tradition pray over the candles? She moves her hands in a beautiful, sacred motion. That movement of benediction must

have been part of an ancient ritual that women, as priest-
esses, performed long before God became only male and
before only men could become priests.

T hen, a cup of wine may be blessed, as are two freshly
baked loaves of challah, or Sabbath bread.

Blessed are heaven and earth, the sources of all life, who
offer us the fruits of the vine. May we find in this act of
drinking the grateful humility to accept all the sorrows and
joys we have been given, and as we drink, may we find rest
for our souls.

Blessed are the sources of life that bring forth grain
from the earth. Blessed is Mother Earth, who offers her
body that we may be fed. May we be nourished, and may
the strength we receive be used to heal ourselves, heal the
earth, and heal all the family of the earth.

What is it
about this twilight hour?
Even the sound
of a barely perceptible breeze
pierces the heart.

—IZUMI SHIKUBO

W e then offer blessings to the children, and to one another. Placing our hand on the head of one we seek to bless,

we offer blessings of peace, well-being, and happiness. Here is the traditional blessing:

> May the Lord bless you and keep you: May the Lord make his countenance shine upon you, and be gracious unto you: May the Lord lift up his countenance toward you and give you peace.

There are many other blessings we can offer those we love. For our children, we may wish them self-knowledge, courage, safety, or joy. For family or friends we may wish wisdom, peace, or love. Any blessing is a gift, and what a lovely moment, to touch the head of our beloved, speak the deepest truth in our heart, and offer it in love.

> May you be at peace. May you be free from suffering. May you be happy. May you be wise. May you feel great love.

If one goes to a Shabbos meal at Sylvia's house, a bowl of small pieces of paper is passed around, and you get to pick a saying from the *dhammapada*—the sayings of the Buddha—and reflect on how that particular scripture speaks to thoughts of your heart at the end of this week. Lately, angel cards have been added to the pile, cards with a single word, such as "peace" or "faith," upon which you can meditate aloud.

Then a grace may be spoken over the meal, offering thanksgiving for all who have come, all who brought the food to our table, those who grew and picked and harvested, those who cooked and cleaned and prepared the food. Then a simple song may be sung. With our voices, our hands, our eyes, all our senses we honor that the time of sacred rest and delight has come.

Don't surrender your loneliness
So quickly.
Let it cut more deep.

Let it ferment and season you
As few human
Or even divine ingredients can.

Something missing in my heart tonight
Has made my eyes so soft,
My voice
So tender,

My need of God
Absolutely
Clear.

— HAFIZ

MORNING

For many, Sabbath mornings begin with some form of worship with others. Jacqueline writes, "For me, the Sabbath began at sunrise on Sunday and walking to church as a family for Mass and communion. I really did love Sundays—we always did things together with both my mother and father, and church was very much a part of this."

When I was sixteen my friends and I rose earlier than most teenagers on a Sunday morning to play at the folk Mass at our local Catholic parish. Some of us, including me, were not even Catholic—but there was something irresistible about playing guitars and singing about peace and love with a church full of hundreds of people, voices harmonizing, and hearts opening. Afterward, we would have lunch with the priest, who took us under his wing, shared off-color stories, and subtly offered a moral teaching presence. Beginning the day with song and communion forever changed for me the feeling of the Sabbath day.

My friend Mary begins her Sabbath with morning prayer. "I go to a table in my living room and light a beautiful candle, inviting the Holy Spirit to come into this day, guiding me and nourishing me. Then I sit quietly for a while, appreciating the beauty of the place, looking at or handling sacred objects on my table. Mostly what I keep are small gifts from people, things that remind me that my presence has mattered, that I have touched people, that I am connected, that I am so incredibly blessed. From there it's journaling—first, dreams, if there have been some remembered, and then whatever seems to be up that morning; it's a way for me to check in with myself and Spirit. When I'm done with the journaling, I do a period of Centering Prayer, and move into the day."

For those who do not attend formal worship, Sabbath morning can be a lazy time, with no place to go and nothing to do. We have seen how couples stay in bed, share stories of their week, confess intimate turnings of the soul, make love, drink champagne, and revel in doing nothing of any consequence—and how Doug Wilson calls this particular spiritual practice "Slotha Yoga."

My friend Nicole says she tries to stay in her pajamas as long as she possibly can. "It is impossible," she says, "to do anything responsible in pajamas."

DEENA METZGER:

> Waking in the morning
> Time smiles in my hand.
> This dawn
> Lasts all day.

Mary is an entrepreneur who started her own business five years ago. As a recovering alcoholic, she threw herself into building a consulting firm that became, through her tireless effort, a successful enterprise. But the cost was a nagging weariness. She would work weekends, taking work home, staying at the office long after dark.

She decided she could not keep up this pace and remain healthy, and she was taking little joy in her success. She stopped working on Sundays, and went to a meditation meeting early in the morning, which became like her church. She took up horseback riding. Now she drives to the country and, for two hours, rides a horse, feeling a gentle melting into contact with horse and earth and movement that soothes and consoles her. "If I don't go to the meditation meeting first, it is a very different ride, more driven, less relaxed. I am still tense when I get on the horse, and the horse can feel it. The horse knows the difference, if I have been to my meeting or not." After two hours of Sabbath riding, Mary feels nourished and refreshed. "I start my week more spaciously, with more ease and delight in my work."

AN OLD HASIDIC POEM:

> Take special care to guard your
>   tongue before the morning prayer.
> Even greeting your fellow, we are told,
>   can be harmful at that hour.
> A person who wakes up in the morning is
>   like a new creation.
> Begin your day with unkind words,
>   or even trivial matters—
>   even though you may later turn to prayer,
>   you have not been true to your Creation.
> All of your words each day
>   are related to one another.
> All of them are rooted
>   in the first words that you speak.

Sunday mornings we gather our children, Sherah and Maxwell, into our bedroom. We sit together in a circle and light a candle, then meditate for about five minutes. We then take turns offering a prayer for someone we are concerned about, and also offer a prayer for something we are thankful for. Some weeks it is poignant and loving, others more silly. Thanks have been given for love and safety as well as for pocketknives and CD's. Finally, we dedicate a certain amount of money from everyone's allowance—usually a few dollars every week—to be given away, and we discuss who we think could most benefit. It is usually up to the children to decide— we merely offer suggestions. The children seem to like this part the best, knowing that someone in the world will receive the blessing of our having sat together for a few moments around a candle in a bedroom.

AFTERNOON

Sabbath afternoons are renowned for their ability to evoke unrepentant napping. Throughout Latin America and Europe, the afternoon nap is sacrosanct; in the United States, we are at least allowed to nap on the Sabbath.

For Janet, walking is her Sabbath meditation. This past season, when her husband ran for governor, their lives were perpetually hectic and rushed, with little time to rest. In the midst of the campaign, she dropped me this note:

During these campaign times (the military meaning is no accident) I find that sitting—even if I force myself to sit for thirty minutes—is ineffective. I just wind up tighter and create more lists. In these times, just walking (which after thirty minutes becomes meditative walking) is the most important and renewing act for me. I like the silence, the air, the feel of the ground under my feet, I like not being enclosed, I like the repetitive movement of my legs. After thirty minutes I begin to walk more softly, my thoughts have spun themselves out and I am walking in the space, I feel the air and sun, I smell the piñon and cedar. My legs move with no noticeable effort. It is a splendid moment which I carry with me and helps when I step back into the whirlwind.

DIANE ACKERMAN:

Although every culture on our planet makes music, each culture seems to invent drums and flutes before anything else. Something about the idea of breath or wind entering a piece of wood and filling it roundly with a vital cry—a sound—has captivated us for a millennia. It's like the spirit of life playing through the whole length of a person's body. It's as if we could breathe into the trees and make them speak. We hold a branch in our hands, blow into it, and it groans, it sings.

Robert writes to tell me about his flute, which has become a Sabbath for him:

For Sabbath time, I play the shakuhachi (Japanese bamboo flute) for at least an hour each day. The practice I follow is called blowing-Zen, becoming Buddha in one sound, bringing one's full attention to each note, rather than cruising through a melody. The music I play comes out of the forests of Japan, from monasteries where monks breathe in the wind-trees-water-birds-animals around them and then breathe them out. In between there is a transformation of presence that is, for me, Beauty itself. It's my friend. We lose ourselves in each other.

For many, music is a language that connects beneath words, deep in the body and heart. For centuries people have used hymns, chants, and sacred melodies to center and attune their souls. One rabbi says that, despite traditional Sabbath prohibitions against using electricity, "I cannot imagine a Sabbath without my stereo. I do not believe God would want me to have a Sabbath without Mahler."

Perhaps the most universally popular Sabbath activity involves going out into nature. Strolling, hiking, lying under a tree, feeling the heartbeat of the earth, the rhythms of nature that synchronize the beating of the heart, the breath in the lung. Joseph, who works very hard, tells me, "The two things I've found most helpful have been times for regular meditation practice and opportunities to play in nature. The first reconnects me with the empty, alive essence of things through the practice of non-doing, and the second helps me feel the vibrant connection of body, mind, and world. Both are great joys."

On the beach, my wife Christine leads us all to a place in the sand where she draws an enormous circle, a mandala. Passing a stick to each of us in turn, Maxwell, Sherah, and I each add a line, a figure, a shape to the mandala. We all take turns several times until the mandala lets us know it is finished. As we stand back and look at what we have done, Christine offers cornmeal to the four directions. The crows sweep down and eat, decorating the mandala with their impossibly black wings.

My dear friend Carolyn, every Sunday afternoon, sits quietly and writes letters. "I have friends I don't get to see, and I love writing letters, the physical touch of pen on paper. I get to spend time with people I love as I think about them, about how they are doing, about what I could share that they would like. It is a little old-fashioned, but that is part of why I like it so much. It connects me to an earlier time, when life was slower, and more thoughtful."

Brenda uses Sabbath afternoons to call friends who live far away. She sets aside time to make long-distance calls, so that she will stay close to those who are separated by miles and time. "It is one of my favorite times," she says. "I do not want to lose the precious gift of these people in my life just because they are far away."

Some, of course, simply pray. Prayer can be spare, unencumbered. In the Christian tradition, centering prayer uses a single, sacred word as an object of meditation. Following the breath, one returns again and again to the sacred word— perhaps *love*, or *peace*, or *mercy*. Using the breath in silent contemplation, a quiet mindfulness arises. This is true prayerfulness; the mind resting gently in the heart. Sabbath is an especially sweet time for giving thanks; we remember all the blessings, gifts, and fruits of our life, and offer a simple word of gratefulness.

LEAVING SABBATH TIME

Traditionally, Sabbath ends after sunset, when three stars become visible in the evening sky. It is useful to leave Sabbath time mindfully, even if a bit reluctantly. Jews have a Sabbath-ending ceremony called *Havdalah*.

For Havdalah, Jacob and his family sit quietly on the floor around the Havdalah candle. They are silent for a moment, and then each shares the best part of Sabbath, and what they look forward to in the week. "It is a time of grounding us together before we go back into our busy lives," he says. "It is a good time to be together."

A cup of spices is passed, the sweet aroma reminding us of the delicious Sabbath time, so that as we leave and reenter the work of our life, we carry with us the lingering fragrance of rest. We do not rush back to work, but rather go leisurely, easily, without hurry or haste. We feel more spacious, and the spices in the nostrils are a sensual reminder of where we have been.

When I am in Alabama, visiting our Birmingham Bread for the Journey chapter, one of the organizers brings me her ceramic Havdalah candleholder, wine goblet, and spice cup. They are made by hand, just as much of Shabbat is made by hand. During our meeting, she passes around the spices. Even as we sit and make plans to serve the poor of the city, we are blessed with the aroma of rest.

Whatever is foreseen in joy
Must be lived out from day to day.
Vision held open in the dark
By our ten thousand days of work.
Harvest will fill the barn; for that
The hand must ache, the face must sweat.
And yet no leaf or grain is filled
By work of ours; the field is tilled
And left to grace. That we may reap,
Great work is done while we're asleep.
When we work well, a Sabbath mood
Rests on our day, and finds it good.

— WENDELL BERRY

Sources and Permissions

Page 169: Lao Tzu. From *Tao Te Ching by Lao Tzu: A New English Version*, with foreword and notes by Stephen Mitchell. Translation copyright © 1988 by Stephen Mitchell. Reprinted by permission of HarperCollins Publishers, Inc.

Page 171: Kenyon, Jane. "Let Evening Come" and excerpt from "Ice Out" copyright © 1996 by the Estate of Jane Kenyon. Reprinted from *Otherwise: New & Selected Poems* by Jane Kenyon with the permission of Graywolf Press, Saint Paul, Minnesota.

Page 192: Ungar, Lynn. "Camas Lilies" from *Blessing the Bread: Meditations* by Lynn Ungar. Boston: Unitarian Universalist Association, 1995.

Page 207: Farley, Morgan. "How to Own Land" from *Saludos! Poemas de Nuevo Mexico: Poems of New Mexico*, selected and edited by Jeanie C. Williams and Victor di Suvero; translations edited by Consuelo Luz. Tesuque, N.M.: Pennywhistle Press, 1995.

Page 221: Hafiz. "Don't surrender your loneliness" from *The Subject Tonight Is Love: 60 Wild and Sweet Poems of Hafiz*, translated by Daniel Ladinsky. Copyright © 1996 by Pumpkin House Press. Reprinted by permission of Pumpkin House Press.

Page 223: Metzger, Deena. "Waking in the morning" from *A Sabbath Among the Ruins*. Copyright © 1992 by Deena Metzger. Berkeley, C.A.: Parallax Press. Reprinted by permission of the author.

Page 224: "An Old Hasidic Poem" from *Your Word Is Fire: The Hasidic Masters on Contemplative Prayer*, translated by Arthur Green and Barry W. Holtz. Woodstock, V.T.: Jewish Lights Books, 1993.

Page 232: Berry, Wendell. "Whatever is foreseen in joy" from *Sabbaths* by Wendell Berry. Copyright © 1987 by Wendell Berry. Reprinted by permission of North Point Press, a division of Farrar, Straus & Giroux, Inc.

Acknowledgments

When I first embarked on this pilgrimage, many people freely offered me the kindness of their loving companionship. Joan Borysenko and Kurt Koltreider, Chris and David Hibbard, Rachel Naomi Remen, Stephen Mitchell, Norman Lear, Mark E. Pollack, Steve and Sybil Wolin, Lynn Willeford, Sharon Salzberg, Achahn Amaro, Janet Quinn, and Teri McLuhan read first drafts or offered helpful suggestions early on. I am especially indebted to Rabbi Zalman Schachter-Shalomi who, along with his wife Eve Ilsen, invited me into their home and their precious library. Many of my approaches to Shabbat took birth in the soil of their fertile wisdom. Any subsequent confusions of interpretation are, of course, my own.

Many generously offered Sabbath stories from their own lives. They are far too numerous to mention by name, and most offered them tenderly, privately. You know who you are, and I thank you. May your lives and your stories give new life to the practice of Sabbath-keeping.

Others have supported me with their own distinctive gifts. Rob Lehman and Molly Vass took me in and offered me their love, and further offered the resources of Sister Gilchrist and the Fetzer Institute; Wink Franklin invited me, and my work, to be part of the family at the Institute of Noetic Sciences; Brother David Steindl-Rast took me on a nourishing walk on a perfect Sabbath afternoon; Trevor Hawkins was there when I most needed him; Jamil Kilbride offered the necessary leavening of irreverent laughter; Katie Olson offered enthusiastic telephonic companionship; Mark Nepo shared his poems, love and doughnuts; Sylvia Boorstein shared delightful lunchtimes at Max's; with Chris Harrington, it was lunch at the Parkside; Susan Jeffers and Mark Shelmerdine provided valuable friendship, hospitality, and sanctuary; Lorraine and Oscar Castro-Neves shared many a meal where we spoke of the beauty of music and rest; Rabbi Nahum Ward-Lev offered his thoughtful support; and Ann and Jim Quinn offered their lovely home for regular retreats, as did my dear friends Kurt Bochner, Deepa Narayan, and John Blaxall. Nella and Steve Abbott shared their lovely beach house, and Don Krawets provided the perfect atmosphere for writing about rest.

I am especially grateful for the growing family of volunteers throughout the country whose natural generosity, lovingly offered to those in need, breathes passion, life, and joy into our Bread for the Journey chapters. Many offer themselves freely and often, and deserve more thanks than I can give them here. Cindy Ward has gone out of her way to serve us at every opportunity. My dear friend Maryanne Finch is a dedicated friend of the poor whose unconditional compassion inspires us always to go a little deeper. I am indebted to Linda Samuels for helping organize my life so that I had time to write, and to Marianna Cacciatore and Anne Fullerton and Julie Daniel for their patience with me as they skillfully guided Bread for the Journey. Ben Whitehill has accompanied me on many Bread for the Journey travels, and helped provide needed support at a critical time; his wife Carolyn supplied many stories and, more importantly, a gentle, loving wisdom that has sustained us for years. Richard Johnson has been an invaluable, delightfully competent friend and colleague who miraculously makes everything we do a little easier.

I thank Dr. Richard Heckler, in part for his friendship of these last twenty-seven years, and especially for the quality of his love for me. It is a gift I cannot imagine living without. As always, I am grateful to Loretta Barrett, who freely gave me her friendship, her faithful support, and her guidance—

qualities that are delightful complements to her expertise as my literary agent. And my editor, Toni Burbank, has a remarkable ability to find the jewel in the lotus, the treasure hidden in the field—or in my case, the needle in the haystack. It was the companionship of her expert ear that allowed me to uncover the music of rest.

Finally, I could not have written this book without the support and understanding of my wife, Christine Tiernan, and my children, Sherah and Maxwell. One cannot reflect on rest without some period of quiet, and they offered me that gift—and so many others—more often than I had the right to expect.

For all the blessings I have received, I thank you all.

About the Author

WAYNE MULLER is an ordained minister and therapist and founder of Bread for the Journey. A graduate of Harvard Divinity School, he is Senior Scholar at the Fetzer Institute and a fellow of the Institute of Noetic Sciences. He also runs the Institute for Engaged Spirituality and gives lectures and retreats nationwide. He is the author of *Legacy of the Heart,* a *New York Times* best-seller, and *How, Then, Shall We Live?* He lives with his family in northern California.

A portion of the proceeds from this book will be used for the work of Bread for the Journey, which supports the efforts of local people serving the poor, hungry, and others in need.

There are now more than twelve chapters of Bread for the Journey nationwide. For locations, and for information about starting a Bread for the Journey chapter in your community, please write or call us:

Bread for the Journey
267 Miller Avenue
Mill Valley, CA 94941
Phone 415-383-4600
E-mail: bread@slip.net
HYPERLINK http://www.breadforthejourney.org

You can also contact us for a list of Wayne Muller's retreats, workshops, books, and tapes.